11:02 AM

To Rick
my new friend and
brother from another
mother. Continue
the journey for truth
and keep your God
given courage

Osei

The Demon Within

A Nation of Addicts

by

Kwame Osei Moyo

Bloomington, IN

Milton Keynes, UK

AuthorHouse™
1663 Liberty Drive, Suite 200
Bloomington, IN 47403
www.authorhouse.com
Phone: 1-800-839-8640

AuthorHouse™ UK Ltd.
500 Avebury Boulevard
Central Milton Keynes, MK9 2BE
www.authorhouse.co.uk
Phone: 08001974150

First published by AuthorHouse 12/11/2006

ISBN: 978-1-4259-7960-7 (sc)

Library of Congress Control Number: 2006910055

Printed in the United States of America
Bloomington, Indiana

This book is printed on acid-free paper.

Acknowledgements

I am not to be confused as a writer as you will discover through reading this book. I did not achieve the education, or literary skills necessary to be a proficient writer. I am, however, a man who suffered with a powerful, totally possessive, and evil disease for over thirty years of my life. I will do my best to be honest about all of it. I owe much of my motivation and courage to write this book to certain individuals that I hold in the highest esteem. Without their leadership, mentoring, and guidance, it would not have been possible. I would like to thank God, my Heavenly Father who is all things to all men. He is Yahweh, Jehovah, Elohim, Moriah, YHWH, JHVH, Yeshua, the Messiah, the Prince of Peace, and Lord of Hosts. He is the Creator of heaven and earth, the Maker of man and mankind, the Giver and Sustainer of life, the Father of time and the Mother of love, compassion, and mercy. He is omnipotent and omnipresent and the heavenly father of Jesus the Christ. I am able to write this book because of God's mercy shown me by saving me from me. This book is written in memory of my beloved mother who taught me to laugh despite all that is going on around me, who worked like a mule to give her children sustenance, shelter, food and clothing. It is written in memory of my wonderful, loving, gentle, caring father who lived with addiction a great portion of his life, enslaved by this demon. I especially thank my daughter, little Levon, for being my friend early on in my recovery. She noticed tears coming from my eyes in church one Sunday, and asked "Daddy, what's wrong?" I told her that it was allergies. She knew better, and held my hand. That was a moment now indelible in my soul. I thank my former wife, Emma, who supplied me with pertinent information, and my extremely talented son, Thomas, the fourth. Thank you, Tyler, my little boy, for being my buddy. (You have tried my patience and tolerance to astronomical levels.). And my daughters Renee and Regina; at last we're reunited. Thank you, my sisters, LaVerne, Gloria, and Eunice, along with my nieces and nephews. Thank you, Dr. Gyasi Foluke, for starting me on this never-ending journey of knowledge, learning and revelations; and Dr. Reginald Hawkins (the Warrior) for having undying faith and unparalleled courage to stand for what you believe. You are truly one of God's chosen ones. My dear Rebecca H, thank you for being a stellar woman and companion to me during some of my most troubled years, and being a child of the LIVING GOD. To Dr Julius Chambers for his tenacity and loyalty to the struggle. I once asked Dr. Chambers about the brothers on the corners of America and what can I do? He simply said, "If nothing more, talk to them." Attorney James Ferguson for his total involvement in the struggle, Jim G for teaching me and being an integral part of my restoration to life, Linda V for being there for me as a friend and more also for being such an excellent example of an astute business woman and confidant; Genial Frazier who has fought tirelessly and who never learned the word "quit," James Barnett, Ted Holmes who was instrumental in encouraging me by example to read tenaciously; my sponsees who are all like the brothers that I never had; the fellowship, my home group, my brothers Wyatt P, Larry M. James W, Deronda M, and all of the members of the world famous HOW group; Rahman Allah for being my friend, Ahmad Daniels for his involvement in the struggle, Cynthia McKinney (one helluva sister with more courage and conviction than Samson), all of my Muslim brothers and sisters "Assalaam Alaikum "to you all, the powerful and fearless, Shaka of the Zulu nation, Ida B Wells, Madame CJ Walker, Nkechi Taifa, Laura Whitethorn, Noah Chomsky, Democracy Now, the ANSWER organization, Move On.org; a brother who leads by example with his undying loyalty, faith and endurance DANNY GLOVER (my biggest hero in life), the

Trans African Movement, Oprah Winfrey, Maya Angelou, the late AL-HAQQ MALIK EL-SHABAZZ aka MALCOLM X, the late Dr. Martin Luther King, the late Medgar Evers, the fearless Crazy Horse (D), Sitting Bull, Gall, Crow King, Hump, Fast Bull, Geronimo, Kicking Bird, Cochise, Tecumseh, Black Hawk, Ten Bears, Marcus Garvey, Harriette Tubman (D), Sojourner Truth (D) Rosa Parks, Mother Teresa, the Dalai Lama, People for Peace; Anita Stroud (D), Hattie Anderson (D), my wonderful deceased father Thomas Clyde Saunders who even with his silence taught me well about character and humility, my hard working mother, Lallage Williams Saunders, who worked hard as a mule to provide sustenance, food and shelter to me and my siblings; Joe Howey, Sr. who taught me about the love, dedication and loyalty to family, Nelson Mandela, Nomzamo Winnifred (Winnie) Mandela, Walter Sisulu, Oliver Tambo; The Nation of the Xhosas, Kwame Toure, Jomo Kenyatta, Fidel Castro for his involvement in Angola, President Daniel Arap Moi of Kenya, past President of Kenya Jomo Kenyatta. The courageous leader of the Congo Patrice Lumumba (assassinated), President Benjamin Mkapa of Tanzania; Kwesi Mfume, President of the Congo Laurent Kabilla (D), Kwame Nkrumah (D), all of my sons, brothers and sisters in the Maasai Mara (Narok Kenya); the nation of the Ashanti, Aprella Bridges, Afranie Toufour (asante sana for the love that you showed me and my daughter while there), Adjua my biggest and most beautiful fan in Kumasi, my son in Accra Atta, Alhaji (my brother in Kumasi, Barbara Lee, Barbara Jordan (D), Shirley Chisholm (D), Maxine Waters, Fannie Lou Hamer (D); Mary McLeod Bethune (D), W.E.B. Dubois (D), Marva Collins, Eleanor Norton Holmes, Marian Wright Edelman a strong woman who truly loves the children and has devoted her life to them, MEL BLOUNT (R Pittsburgh Steelers) for his unselfish work towards starting a boy's home for troubled youth (a big unsung hero of mine asante sana Mel), Michael Moore; Tim Wise, Morris Deese (these three very brave white men I love and respect); The CURE organization- Donna Rice- Larry Yates- Dorothy Blake Fardan-Molly Secours- Jerry Saltzman- Ida Hakim- Amy Kedron- Carol Chehade- Mark George and all other CURE members, Minister Clifford Jones (for being such an honest and dedicated leader in the Charlotte area, a

God fearing man and pastor of The Friendship Missionary Baptist Church (thank you Pastor Jones)- Charlotte, NC; Reverend Ricky Woods, Don Stegers of the Reeder Memorial Baptist Church who delivered such a powerful message on Drifting in the wrong direction" on April 30, 2006; Fannie Waterman for her incredible courage who was instrumental in her walk through the hatred going to class on the first day, Dorothy Counts for her courageous walk being the first Black student enrolled at Harding High School and enduring the hatred and taunts); the warrior and courageous Angela Davis, all of the ministers who were involved in the struggle, the teachers who showed unconditional love to us back in the daze, the Attorneys that were involved in the struggle, the Southern Poverty Law Center; the lay people and to all of my beloved Black people for being my brothers and sisters (the salt of the earth), all of the Black and White kindred spirits of the world who want to help but don't know how, simply read, speak and practice "truth" and teach your children about the Great Nile Valley Civilization (the first), Caesar Chavez; and last but not least Ann Graham (an angel at Little Rock AME Zion Church) and her crew who helped so selflessly to feed the 10,000 the first year and for continuing to feed the sheep. I would also like to thank the three lambs of God who were brutally slaughtered in Philadelphia Mississippi for their God given beliefs. These workers were Michael "Mickey" Schwerner, Andrew "Andy" Goodman, and James "J.E." Chaney. These people exhibited thankless service, love, and leadership in some dangerous times. Some of them I encountered on the journey through books and historical documents, they encouraged me, inspired me and taught me about unconditional love. All of them lifted me up to total involvement in the struggle. Angela Davis spoke these words, "Revolution is a serious thing, the most serious thing about a revolutionary's life. When one commits oneself to the struggle, it must be for a lifetime."

Asante Sana to you all.
Kwame Osei Moyo

Foreword

It was drizzling rain on Wyatt Street and it was dark. I heard someone yell "NIGGER YOU PICKED OUT YOUR PLOT YET?" It was unusual even though I knew this was street talk. It sounded somewhat frightening; maybe it was the tone of the voice. I discounted it as the usual BS you hear in the streets; I figured they were just joking. I was also waiting for my runner to bring a package back since you'd "better" know somebody if you knock on the door of a cop house or you could wind up dead. The windshield wipers made their monotonous sound of Splish Splop splish splop with a squeaking sound they emit when the window's mostly dry. I was almost dozing off to the sounds of Earl Klugh playing My funny Valentine" when I heard these loud BOOM BOOM BOOM BOOM BOOM. I jumped and my heart started racing so fast I thought I may have a heart attack. It was a barrage of gunfire so loud , it almost scared me to death. I knew these had to be big guns that seemed from the flash to be aimed directly at me. He dropped like a sack of potatoes in front of me. I started hyperventilating so bad the windshield started fogging up. There was no doubt that he was dead before he hit the ground. OH MY GOD! I had just witnessed a murder; I was terrified! What if they saw me? I knew they would not let me escape being a witness. I started the car and slid straight out waiting for another blast to come through my windshield and find it's mark...ME. I left and never looked back. I knew beyond the shadow of a doubt that the cops would be there very soon followed by the press with cameras. Death was kind this time in the world of drugs, violence and murder!

And so it began: the explosive and powerful story of one prominent Charlottean's experience with the demon named Addiction, and his spiral descent into the dark abyss of hell. It speaks of the mental, spiritual, and emotional torture of drug addiction and how it destroys everything. This graphic and detailed story addresses some of the most common misconceptions about drugs and addiction. It details the culture, and dangers associated with the disease and a lifestyle that often involve homicides and suicides.

I will share with you the colorful portrait of my own life from early childhood through the ranks of Corporate America. Ultimately, I will share my head first fall from the rungs of the business world to the dungeons of total despair, shame, and isolation from society and family. Finally, after reaching a point of desperation and hopelessness, I called on God Almighty to save my life and sanity. To give up would have meant the eventual loss of my life through suicide.

This book also presents facts about the effects of the most satanic and evil practice known to man, called racism, and how this evil affects some of its victims. Sometimes these facts are hard and distasteful. But I hope they will help you understand racism's profound impact on addiction, society, and our children.

I hope the book states clearly and loudly why Black men in this society are becoming extinct—same as the dinosaur. Please, carefully absorb every word and every line of "The Demon Within: A Nation of Addicts."

Finally, and above all, this autobiography is written as the last act of purging my soul. Beyond that, it is for all of mankind: theologians, housewives, mothers, fathers, husbands, teachers, physicians, judges; members of law enforcement, behaviorists, intellects, laymen, the medical community; administrators in the penal system, people of all races, creeds and national origins; for the elderly, the socialites, the wealthy, the inmates, friends of the court, engineers, architects; especially for athletes, entertainers,

musicians, teenagers, criminals, gangsters, and all that live and breathe in this society or any other.

It is written from the depths of my heart for the still suffering addict. For them it is a hand showing a way out of the mental anguish and the suffering of Hell's chambers.

Asante Sana to you all.
Kwame Osei Moyo

"There is no easy walk to freedom anywhere, and many of us will have to pass through the valley of the shadow of death again and again before we reach the mountaintop of our desires."

Nelson Mandela

Chapter One - The Beginning

February 3, 1935. Colored baby girl born to father Jesse Lomax age eighteen and mother Lallage Williams age sixteen. Charlotte, NC.

Baby girl named La Verne Williams. June 12, 1943. Colored baby girl born to father Thomas Clyde Saunders age 41 and the mother Lallage Williams Saunders age 24.

Baby girl named Gloria Ann Saunders. January 9, 1945. U.S. Forces land on Luzon, Philippines. World War Two.

January 12, 1945. Russians open winter offensive with remarkable progress. WWII.

January 13, 1945. Colored baby boy, Thomas Clyde Saunders, II, born at Good Samaritan Hospital. The father Thomas Clyde Saunders age forty-three and the mother Lallage Williams Saunders age twenty-six.

January 14, 1945. Death marches to the interior of Germany begin, taking 250,000 Jewish lives. Death Camps

August 6, 1945. The first atomic bomb is dropped on Hiroshima, an explosion equal to 20,000 tons of TNT.

August 9, 1945. A second atomic bomb is dropped on Nagasaki; Soviets declare war on Japan, attacking Manchuria.

August 14, 1945. End of the war with Japan.

June 14, 1947. Colored baby girl named Eunice Lallage Saunders born to father Thomas Clyde Saunders 45 and mother Lallage Williams Saunders age 28.

"Do you solemnly swear that the testimony you are about to give this court is the truth, the whole truth and nothing but the truth so help you God?"

"I do."

Sometime in 1946: Voice #1: Dat youngun's got rickets, Lal. Voice #2: Whies dat youngun so red chile? Voice #3: You need to fatten dat youngun up honey, he's a runt. Mostly, I remember voices, not faces. Not names, but voices. My mother's name was Lallage. Rather than get it wrong, everyone called her Lal. Certain things I remember; most things I don't. The fuzzy things my sisters, Gloria and LaVerne, helped me with. If I live to be 1200 years old, I'll never understand how in the world women can remember things from 300 years ago; the color dress "that woman" had on, her blouse and shoes; men can't remember what they had for breakfast. 333 Earle Street is where we lived for the first four or five years of my life. These were government projects we've come to know as planned slums. The first two years of my life were spent listening, learning, and probably babbling what infants and toddlers babble. The weather back then was what it should have been—hot in the summer, and cold in the winter. As hot as it was in August, I could never understand how the neighborhood women wouldn't faint doing all of that work. They had very strict work ethics and would finish the day's chores if it dragged on through the night. It seems that during those hot summers, they were always sweating from working in the house, washing clothes, cooking, ironing, plaiting hair, and finally giving baths to all the children sufficiently fed and tired from a hard day's play.

The women always carried, or found something to fan themselves as the sweat poured down their bodies. Sometimes they would come over to our house, collapse in a comfortable chair, and melt into it. Thank God for those window fans. "Whew chile, sho is hot, Lal. Brang me a glass of water, honey." "Hot enuf to fry aigs on de sidewalk, betta have sum shoes on yo feet; you shoa git blisters."

"Hmpph! Burn yo feet sumpin bad. Dat hardheaded youngun of mine ran out wid no shoes on his feet de udder day. Honey, when he hit dat sidewalk he tap-danced all the way back here screaming and hollering. Blisters all over his feet. He keeps shoes on now even in the house, don't wanna take em off even when it's bedtime."

These were the days before TV when people talked to each other and were in and out of each other's houses daily. The village was so much closer and smaller, was much more like one big family. There was no knocking on doors, you would just walk in and yell your presence. We had everything in the village—mostly each other. We had everything except the ancestral drums.

The men worked like mules at their jobs and were dog-tired and hungry when they came home. There was never a question about food being "ready" when anyone's daddy came home. Most of them were street workers who repaired the potholes with that hot, hot asphalt. Some were cooks, yard workers, garbage men, construction workers, and so on.

My daddy's drinking was a part of him. I'm sure that some of the men had a nip when they got home to relax them a little. Some didn't touch the stuff at all until the weekend. My daddy was different. I remember him smelling like alcohol daily. It smelled stronger on the weekends. I remember him picking me up in his arms sometime when he was feeling good.

The drinking progressed the same as any other chronic disease as time went by, and somehow I knew that he had a problem. What that problem was I had no idea but I knew that if the problem would leave, things would be different.

Daddy was a quiet man far back as I can remember. He was a distinguished looking man, a good man, and I loved him. His complexion was always reddish. I'm told my daddy's mother or grandmother was Cherokee. I was proud of this because today I know that these were some of the most spiritual people that ever lived. I've never seen photos of my daddy's parents nor have I ever met them. I always wondered what they looked like, where they were from. We never talked about them. I realize today how important it is to know your history and especially your lineage. Such secrets are destructive to our spiritual and mental well-being.

Malcolm X said, "History is a people's memory, and without memory man is demoted to the lower animals." I know today that when we came to this country under the threat of torture and death that the greatest loss was not life and limb, nor being whipped brutally and mercilessly, nor having our native tongues and religious beliefs taken away. The greatest tragedy we experienced was the loss of our identity. Nothing is worse than a man who doesn't know who he is. When a man is stripped of his heritage, dignity, and self worth, he automatically seeks something to soothe the pain and comfort his spirit, even if only temporarily. This loss of identity is one of the main reasons that addiction is greater in the Indigenous Americans, Black, and Latino communities. It's because many of us don't know who we are.

My father would be referred to today as a kindred spirit. He would give you his last. He was the most humble man I knew. He was never loud or arrogant even when he was drinking

He and I had a spiritual connection early on. I was the only one who truly understood him, even at an early age. Momma knew that he was a good man as well and could only fuss about his drinking. I would find out later that Daddy and I would have more in common than earlier thought.

I was a very quiet little boy who, sometimes during rain or snowstorms, would gaze out of the window. I enjoyed the peace and silence of falling snow, especially in the early mornings when no one had awakened but me. Snow doesn't make a sound when it's falling. No thunder, no lighting and in some cases, no howling wind.

I was always thinking, trying to put things together. I wondered who makes the snow, how it forms, and why is it always white? It was a beautiful sight; except when it started melting it became a mess. That once beautiful snow would mix with the dirt and become mud. The muddy water flowed down the street drains and became dirty and ugly.

I often wondered where people go and where they sleep if they're homeless? The notion of homelessness was a mystery to me because only a few homeless people were visible. Families in our community did a much better job of taking care of family members who were not functional or had special needs. I wondered how lonely and uncomfortable it must have been to not have a warm bed to sleep in. Did homeless people have a special place to go where there were beds and food? How did they bathe and go to the bathroom? Most importantly: why did no one seem to care about them? I wondered how homeless people could sleep out in the elements. I was attracted to these people at a very young age. Often times, when my buddies and I were out playing, we would see a homeless person. They smelled bad, were bedraggled with torn and tattered clothes. I would sometimes turn around and stare at them as if I knew their plight, as if I knew what had happened to them. "C'mon man, that's a bum," one of my friends would say. All I saw was someone who had no place to stay and no one to take care of them. I wondered why they always looked down and so sad. I thought about it for a minute and said to myself "I'd be sad too if I had to walk all day because I had nowhere to go. Where could I go if I had no home."

Our house smelled of smoke from coal and wood burning in the winter. There was a stove in the kitchen and the cramped living room. I thank God for them both because without them, we were in trouble. At this point we were less fortunate, some people call it poor, but we didn't know it; at least we kids didn't know. Stoves were a way of life for everyone so it was no big deal. The wood-burning stove was the only source of heat and means of cooking that we had. Mama cooked every bean known to man: lima, pinto, black eyed, navy, great northern, butter, and green beans. It seemed there were beans in a pot every day. The smell of pinto beans was a permanent fragrance in the house. It was like ghetto incense.

Maybe twice a week or so, there would be some sort of meat. We had oatmeal or grits most days for breakfast. One of my favorite meals to this day is potatoes and onions fried together: country style potatoes, we called them.

The iceman delivered fifty-pound blocks of ice for a quarter to keep the iceboxes cool on those sweltering, humid days. The produce man would come around on his raggedy truck to sell fresh vegetables directly from his garden for pennies. That old truck sounded like a western shoot out scaring people to death. That baby would backfire, leaving a trail of smoke. It even had the dogs running for cover.

On Sundays, chickens didn't stand a chance. There was always a foot race and the chickens ran for their very lives; a race they always lost. The sistas had a strategy, just like a boxer with the head fakes. They would look like they were darting in one direction to fool the chicken into running the other way. The poor chicken always ran right into their hands. The winner would go to work methodically. In a twist of the wrist, she'd wring the chicken's neck to take off his head. Then he was dropped in scalding water to get the feathers off. Further down the assembly line, they would be cleaned, quartered, seasoned, and floured. At that point, he was formally introduced to Crisco or, depending on the household's budget, lard. These bad boys were as fresh as it got because they were killed within an hour of their grand appearance at the dinner table.

I could drink almost a full glass of lemonade at one time.

"Junior, stop drinking so fast befoe it comes outta your ears," mama would say.

Being a kid, I sometimes would forget to breathe when drinking. I could slurp louder than any kid in the neighborhood mostly from breathing so loud after nearly losing all of my breath. The lemonade was never cold because there was only one piece of ice in it that had been chipped off the block. For a long time I believed that nothing on God's green earth tasted better than the lemonade these sisters made back in the days. It was a real treat on those hot, summer days when folk were sweating bigtime.

The food tasted so good because every child seemed to stay hungry all the time at least me and my sisters did. The word finicky eater was unheard of. A sibling would snatch your food before you saw the hand coming if you were slow eating.

Back then was as close to heaven as I thought I would ever get. The aroma alone of food cooking was enough to literally stop a person in their tracks. It would be on like a neck bone. Speaking of neck bones, these were a delicacy. Momma would clean those babies good, chop up plenty of onions and a little celery, season, and cook them for at least an hour. She would make a thickener with flour and let everything marinate together. She would then serve this over rice, and fry some johnnie cakes. This combination was better than filet mignon. This meal absolutely excelled with polk salad. I don't know whether the food was that great, or if the cook's love for the village was what flavored it. That village, once strong, loving and caring, has greatly eroded today.

I remember some of the neighbors that lived in the same Project as we did. There were the Roseboros, the Duncans, Ms. Rivers, and a real life angel that God almighty sent as a guardian over us all. Ms. Anita Stroud was as close to a saint as I'll ever know. She lived on the end of the row of projects. She loved all of us kids from the depths of her saintly heart. She was the only person with courage enough to face White folk, and humility enough to plead for money to take us on trips. Ms. Stroud would look them dead in the eye and tell them, "these chilluns ain't never been nowhere and never will without help, and y'all know that we ain't got NUTHIN."

My sister Gloria tells me that Ms Stroud somehow raised enough money to take the neighborhood kids on a bus trip to Boone, NC. I don't remember going; maybe I was too young.

I can remember her talking to me and patting my head while I ate and drank whatever she offered. Ms. Stroud did something that I wasn't accustomed to; she would hold my hand and give me a big hug. I'm not talking about a little namby-pamby hug. Hers was a smothering hug that made me feel good all over. She was always telling me to be a good boy. I believe this had a big effect on me for the rest of my life.

My Grandfather and his two sisters

My no nonsense Grandma

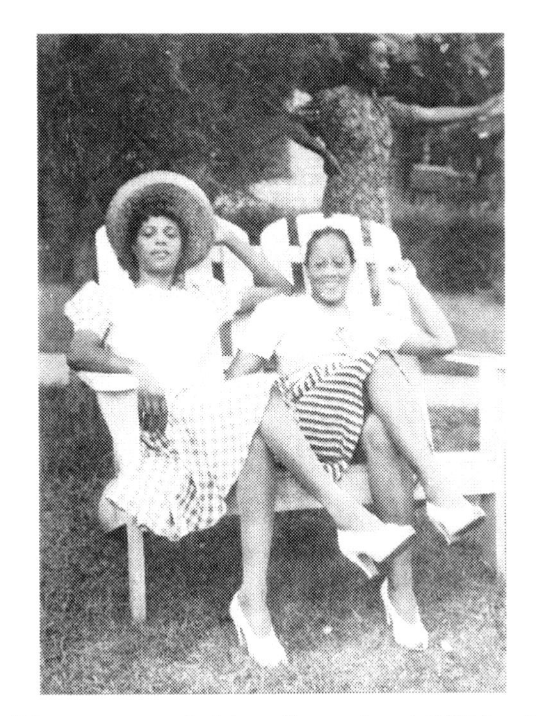

Momma on right and my Aunt Mildred

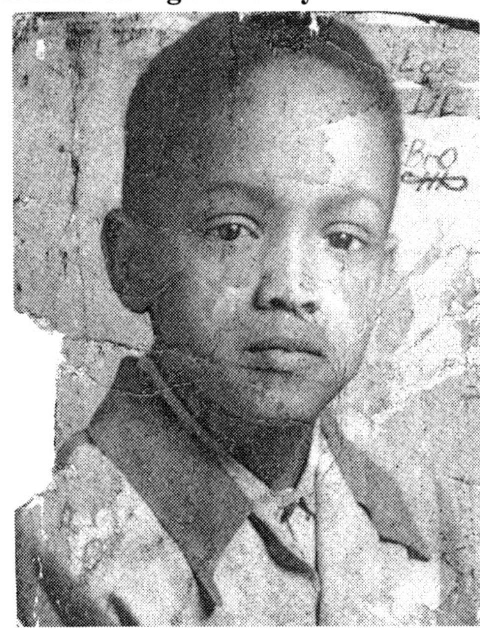

Me at 5 years old (first grade)

Cousin Robert and Sasha

Sasha - 3rd from left and her family in Hiroshima

Graduation 1962 West Charlotte Senior High School

Harry and Irene

Chapter Two - Ms Hattie Anderson-Fairview Elementary School

The other saint of my life was Ms. Hattie Anderson. She was one of my grade school teachers and a legend in her own time. She was the strongest woman spiritually and mentally that I've ever met. But she was beyond the shadow of a doubt the meanest looking person I've ever known.

Ms. Anderson instilled values and integrity in us young children. If you ever thought of telling a lie to Ms Anderson, you knew that your life was in danger. She was totally no-nonsense and quite serious. If you insisted on acting the fool, eventually you would have to learn sign language because she would leave you senseless after a good backside beating. She not only would wear your ass out, she would almost knock your lungs out when she hit you in the back for foolishness. We all learned quickly not to even breathe loud in her class. God forbid that you would have a suspicious grin on your face. She would come directly to your desk, tower over you, and give you a deadly stare. This scared some children almost to tears.

To my recollection, Ms Anderson was the first known terrorist that I knew. She didn't have any weapons of mass destruction but she had very large hands that could hurt a three hundred pound man. There was no doubt that she loved us very much. When she had reason to believe that a student was either sick or sad about something, her words were, "look at me, chile," in a very soft tone. When she looked in a child's eyes, she knew if she had been crying or was afraid. She would oftentimes hug that child and assure him that everything was going to be all right. But if some bully was to try and jump on you, all you'd have to do is say "I'm gon tell Ms Anderson on you." There was always an immediate peace summit. There was not a bully bad enough to challenge Ms Anderson on any day.

When she died some time back, it was truly one of the saddest days in Charlotte for her former students. We will always miss the Hattie Andersons of the world. There was no mistreatment of children in school back then; we were taught by people who loved and understood us. These teachers were all black people who endured the same treatment that we all did on a daily basis. There were no problems of any magnitude in school because we were obedient children who respected authority and harbored a healthy amount of fear as well. There were occasional bullies who sometimes would try the other kids.

I was hassled for a very brief time until my security squad found out about it. I was one smart kid who eventually established a secret service squad. I gained favor by helping the bullies and bad kids to spell, add or anything else. In return, they gave me good backup. I learned early in life to make the bullies your friend, that way no one else dared bother you. If they did, they would face the wrath of Fat Daddy, Long Head Gates, and the bad boys from Fairview Homes.

One day, five girls all of a sudden had a bright idea. They really thought they were bad. They had formed this so-called gang of five. They would intimidate other young girls and make them cry from fear. On this particular day they made a great mistake. They attempted to jump on my big sister, Gloria. Even kids in kindergarten knew better than this. How they missed this fact, I will never know. Gloria Saunders could hurt a grown man. Sis tossed all five of them around like rag dolls and literally beat the living hell out of them. It looked like a cartoon in progress—the one represented by people rolling around with stars, dust, and smoke coming from the fracas. This fight looked like that. The fortunate ones were those who shagged ass when she tossed them aside. After that episode, Gloria had her own security squad because they became her best friends. No one ever tried my sister again. Being Gloria's friend gave even the boys a sense of security. I believe one of those girls started running track in later years because she discovered how fast she could run when my sister let her go.

Chapter Three - Church Going

We went to Church every Sunday. There was no such thing as not feeling good because a big dose of castor oil was the cure for everything. My siblings and me learned that, even when you felt bad on Sunday, you didn't dare tell momma because you were still going to church and get castor oil too. At church, everybody would always sit in the same seat every Sunday. We always sat in front of this large lady who would always start screaming and swinging before she started shouting. I was always in the line of fire because my little head barely came above the pew. Unless I was quick, I'd get clobbered by those large ham hock arms. It was a ritual "every" Sunday, and I had her shouting timed to within five minutes, ducking her every time. It took Gloria longer to figure it out so she got the brunt and the full force of those very large hamhocks.

Reverend Kennedy would preach and preach, and the sweat poured. He was soaking wet when he finished. The ushers kept smelling-salt to bring the sisters around when they passed out from shouting. After church we walked home hungry, ready for dinner. It took momma another thirty minutes to finish cooking. It was normally prepared before we went to church so all she had to do was to warm it up. Over time, Momma had preachers over sometimes and cooked them dinner. It seems like they were all bald with big bellies. The big belly was likely because the preacher usually got the best food when he visited anyone's house for dinner. I hated to see those big belly preachers coming because that meant we children had to wait until they finished before we could eat. It seemed like a week because they would do a lot of talking and leave a lot of damage to the food. There was nothing left of the chicken but the backs and necks. If I had had a mean dog, I would have let him loose on that hungry ass preacher when I saw him coming.

Nights were quiet, only the little sounds of darkness made by frogs and crickets could be heard. There was no traffic or sirens. There was no such thing as streetwalkers, and even the few drunks stayed in at night. Things were so different. I never heard a gun shot when I was a little boy. My two sisters and I slept in the same room. I'll bet there were fewer than six homicides a year in Charlotte back then. Now there are hundreds a year. Doors were never locked, no need to. Folk didn't steal in the village. During the hot summer nights, you could sleep on the steps or outside without worry. It was a disgrace to have a child out of wedlock, and in most cases, the girl would be sent to a relative or elsewhere to have the child and stay for about a year. Everyone honored the village and the villagers. There was respect and compassion for everyone.

If you ever thought of answering an adult with anything except yes sir or yes ma'am, your physical well-being was in danger. The very least I could expect from momma was a good backhand with deadly accuracy that she said would slap you into tomorrow. Back then, children were seen and not heard.

If anyone—child, man, or woman—were sick, the neighborhood would bring homemade tonics, herbs, and woolen rags to heat until the patient was hot as hell. They would tie a poultice around the neck. If the sick ones survived the torturous smell and other remedies, they were always better for it. Afterwards, a potion of tea made from God-knows-what, drank over the next two to three days, always worked without fail.

On many occasions these shaman sisters would sit with the sick until the patient felt better and were able to function again. If you were a child whose mother was afflicted, you could expect to have anyone give you your bath, or make you ready for school.

There were no charts on the wall with ten or twelve hairstyles to choose from. For the boys, it was a soup-bowl-over-the-head haircut. It was plaits for the girls—same style—period. My sisters would scream because the plaits were so tight, they should have lasted for a year. The women would cook enough food to feed their family and the family of whoever was sick.

Being in the care of one of these women changed my life. I'll never forget that day. In the brutal cold of winter, my sister, Gloria, being only five and a half years old, walked us to Ms. Bangum's house. Ms. Bangum kept us during the day while my parents were at work. The snow was up to my knees and my feet were so cold that I couldn't feel them. Gloria carried Eunice, the youngest child, on her back. It was the custom in every family that the oldest girl was delegated the most work and responsibility for the other siblings. We had to make that mile walk back home every day in that brutally cold weather. She had to be exhausted at the end of the journey. Her day seemed to never end. Looking back, I can see why she developed resentment. I seem to remember her crying sometime because, in essence, she never had a childhood. She was either bathing us, plaiting Eunice's hair, ironing, or washing clothes, and the list goes on and on. She told me that she stood on a stool to cook and wash dishes.

Anyway, at Ms. Bynum's house, unlike the food at other homes in the community, the black-eyed peas were always lukewarm and the cornbread was hard enough to scrub pots with. The menu never changed to my recollection. It was during one of these visits that an older neighborhood boy who lived a few doors down molested me. I couldn't have been more than three or four years old. I remember being forced to do things that were beyond my knowledge. I can still vividly see doing things that I didn't want to do. I carried a deep hatred for this guy for decades. As young as I was, I remember the shame and guilt associated with this event that would haunt me for many decades to come.

It was New Year's Eve and daddy was throwing firecrackers out of the door. Daddy was definitely in good spirits and we were having a good time. Then daddy had a bright idea. He let me hold a firecracker to throw out the door. Things didn't go according to plan and that bad boy exploded in my hand. You should have been there. I screamed at the top of my lungs. It seems that I cried a whole week's worth in ten minutes. God, it hurt; my finger was throbbing and the pain was unbelievable.

Momma raised hell with daddy because, once again, he was drunk. I knew that daddy didn't mean the firecracker to explode in my hand. He looked so sad and was full of remorse. I would look into his eyes and see the hurt and disappointment, the hopelessness of not measuring up.

The neighbors ran over and came through that door like a swat team. They must have thought I was being murdered. When they came through that door, wide hips and all, they were prepared for all-out warfare. Daddy couldn't run; he was surrounded. Being cornered, his eyes got bigger. He never heard the end of that story for years to come.

"Chile, you shoulda taken dat frying pan and knocked hell out of em. Shudda worked on dat haid," they told mama.

Daddy became silent. He knew the sistas weren't just upset, they were mad as hell. Don't forget, I was "their" child too. The neighbors loved you almost as much as they loved their own kids. They would whup your butt, tell your momma about it and what you did to earn it. You'd better have a "real good" lie or explanation as to why you did what you did or you would face part two of this episode of a good ass whupping. In most instances you would lose the case every time and there were no appeals. I was always liked as a child, and to my regret I was my mother's favorite.

During that time, there were no drugs—to my knowledge—so alcohol was the drug of most. I don't remember seeing so much as a bottle of liquor, but daddy wore the evidence that one existed somewhere. He left that day and must have returned to the only thing he knew to drown his misery of failing as a husband and father. For the most part, my father stayed drunk on the weekends and simply did the best he could with what he had. He was not a violent man. I thank God that wasn't a part of my story. He always looked at his children with love in his eyes. He never laid a hand on my mother, mainly because she didn't play that. I remember only once he tried to yank her by the arm during an argument. Momma told him to stop twice and then momma actually took a frying pan and hit daddy over the head. As God is my witness, daddy started speaking in another language for four or five minutes. We never till this day figured out what that language was. He never repeated that mistake again.

Like him, other men tried to shield their families from every sin that was fervently preached to them on Sunday mornings. Only a few neighborhood drunks would stagger down the street on the weekends. We children laughed and thought it was funny. There were no meetings for alcoholics. If there were, they certainly would not welcome a Black man in their fold. Today I can see how sad and humiliating life must have been for them. They were suffering from an undiagnosed disease, and suffered greatly as a result. I came to know how their families and loved ones felt.

I learned humiliation firsthand the day that I stood buck naked in front of three or four of the neighbors. Momma had summoned the entire commission to examine me. This was the neighborhood counsel. I held my little head down the whole time looking at the floor. I couldn't have been more than three years old at the time. More voices: Voice#1: "Chile what's wrong with dat younguns peanie? It's swollen" Momma: "I know it. That's why I called yall over to see what's wrong." Voice#2: "Look at dat thang, Lal."Momma: "What do you think I should do?" Voice#3: "Humph, leave it alone. He gon' be a blessing to some woman one day." Loud laughter.

I only remember Black folk during those early days. We were totally separated from Whites and lived in areas known as slums—which were planned by design. The only time I saw a white person was when some insurance man came to the house and sat on the arm of the sofa smoking a cigarette. He flicked the ashes on the floor and put it out in whichever dinner plate was the closest. I immediately started to dislike White people because this one had absolutely no respect for my family and our home. Momma didn't allow us to sit on the arm of any chair in the house but this White man thought that he had the right to do whatever he pleased. I would see this disrespect increasingly unfold throughout my life.

As I became a little older, I started listening and comprehending events and things going on in Charlotte or at least the Black community. The news in those days was humdrum because the crime rate was so incredibly low. I started hearing about Negroes being shot dead by some racist cop claiming self-defense. I also overheard the women talking about how bad they beat him knowing they were talking about some defenseless and scared Black person or youth. I also knew they were talking about the police. The few times I saw the police it was something horrifying about their steely grey or blue eyes that seemed so evil and satanic and full of hatred.

Chapter Four - Growing Up

The fog truck came. It blew out a thick white smoke that I found out later was DDT. I never knew why it came but someone said they sprayed for mosquitoes and whatever. Today, I know that was part of the great lie. We were thought to have lice. I'll never know how we survived that pesticide without contracting major respiratory ailments. I'll never figure out how in creation we were the first family in the Fairview Homes to have a black and white television. But momma was a hustler and had ways to make money. She would have fish fries and sell a little liquor as well. In the summer, every weekend brought the aroma of fried fish in the air. The women would alternate on who was giving the fish fry. Momma sometimes cooked for those big-bellied preachers during the week and charged them. She counted every nickel and dime. All the neighbors would come over and watch Amos and Andy, The Little Rascals and the news on our TV. We laughed so hard at the three Stooges and Amos and Andy. Our home became an unofficial meeting place. Me and the other kids in the neighborhood became cowboys and Indians, playing and having a ball. We had cap pistols and would make bow and arrows. Kids today play with the real deal.

I'll never forget my life at 333 Earle St in the Fairview homes off Oaklawn Avenue. Eventually, We moved. I think the vegetable man came with that raggedy truck and made four trips to take our things to Wyatt Street. The kids walked because it was only four blocks away. The first thing that greeted us when we moved in was the coal stove;

it was always a part of our lives. I didn't know it but the village I had known and trusted till then was beginning to unravel. The distance within the four blocks from Fairview Homes may as well been the other side of the world. We found ourselves among professional folk. And I came to see my family and my life through their passionate eyes. Most of these folk were good people only we were'nt as close as the neighbors on Earle Street. People started staying a little more to themselves, no walking in people's homes anymore. This was a much more formal neighborhood. The kindergarten was half a block up the street. I'll never forget the chocolate milk and graham crackers. They were good and so were our teachers. While only blocks away from Earle Street, this was a much better neighborhood. On Wyatt Street were teachers, and a family that owned their own dry cleaning service and real homes. Wyatt Street ran parallel to Double Oaks Road and Edwin Street. Edwin Street was the cutoff for Fairview Homes. I remember the Granger's, the Platt's, the Shadd's, and my Aunt Madge (the Babbs). My Aunt Madge was a nurse and definitely considered a professional. Ms. Reid and Ms. Shadd were teachers. None of these people had fish fries; they were doing okay.

Double Oaks was a Project of apartments built on a landfill. It's amazing that the residents didn't develop cancer, leukemia, and other ailments. Some of them still live there atop the roller coaster hills that developed as a result on being on very unstable ground and garbage settling. I'm surprised that there's never been a methane gas explosion; but I'm convinced that it's only a matter of time before it happens. We kids loved walking across this Double Oaks playground. One day I could have sworn that I had the discovery of a lifetime. This black stuff that looked like oil was oozing out of the ground. I was already planning what I was going to do with all of that money. I would get an attorney and have them call Exxon to purchase my discovery. I'd get millions upon millions of dollars and buy my mother a big house. I'd give money to my sisters and have my daddy go somewhere to have his drinking problem fixed. Talk about a fairytale. I was more excited than I'd ever been. I was doing all I could not to spill the beans to anyone. I wanted to wait until I had a chauffeur, and a big limousine to ride around in so my friends could all see me. I would be the richest kid in America. I thanked

God for this precious discovery and newfound wealth. I knew that with enough faith and patience that a good kid such as me would be rewarded for being a good kid. I was so happy.

But talk about a letdown. I found out that this stuff was toxic waste that had been dumped there for who knows how long before finally surfacing. This is definitely when I learned to cuss. I cussed a blue streak and and made up a few new words. Until this day nothing was ever done about it. I found out in years to come that whites always dump their waste and trash in "our" neighborhoods with the same consequences and that's always been absolutely nothing said or done to the perpetrators. Life wasn't always bad but somehow it was not as happy inside of our home as it was outside. We kids always found ways to amuse ourselves. We flew kites that we made from newspapers and reeds. We looked for tadpoles in Double Oaks Creek (the colored boys creek). We played in that creek up until the day we saw turds floating in it. We found out later that the guilty culprit was one of the kids we were swimming with. I think that I bathed for an hour that day. It's amazing that I wasn't white when I finished.

Double Oaks School was very close to where we lived. I will never forget the day that I asked momma what we were taking to school for lunch. She started crying. I asked, "What's wrong momma?" "Go over there," she said, pointing to Mrs. Granger's, the house on the right of us, "and ask her if she can give you and your sister something for lunch. Ask nice, now." I was so young but I remember the shame and embarrassment of begging. I promised God and every one of his Disciples on that day, at that moment that I would NEVER, EVER be poor, and have to ask anyone for anything again. Shortly after, I became fully acquainted with the concept of crime. I discovered that whites have all the power, all the money and all the resources—most of which was stolen from Blacks—and I would put my knowledge to use trying to get some of it back, "by any means necessary."

I began to help my mother as much as I could because daddy was spending more of his money on liquor trying to escape his shame, and we were getting bigger as children, and eating more. We didn't approach my Aunt for help because that was too degrading. All the same, I guess she helped to her extent of willingness. She and her husband were part of the elite in the community. I had become aware of how we were treated by those outside our community because we were black. Now I would learn discrimination because we were poor. This damage is doubly painful when it comes from your own people. Because of daddy's drinking, we were more tolerated than accepted, and regarded as a source of embarrassment by some of our relatives. In addition to the nurse, two other of his sisters were teachers. Because alcoholism was regarded as a moral dilemma, we were definitely disenfranchised and disowned by this new village.

My mother was the misfit of her family as well. She had had a child out of wedlock She had been sent to Shelby, NC to live for a while before LaVerne, her firstborn, came into the world. I only saw my oldest sister periodically because she was raised by gran'ma and gran'daddy, as was the custom for a child out of wedlock. Now, it is considered a badge of honor to be a single parent. LaVerne was a beautiful child and young lady. She has natural hazel eyes. Her hair is a color between auburn and brunette. She is very fair and has a light complexion. Gloria's hair is absolutely beautiful—wavy and black. My sister Eunice and I had "nappy" hair. I see the sistas with the locks and dreads today and totally admire their nappy, and natural beautiful hair.

Lunch at school was a welcome time of the day. As Daddy's addiction worsened, we children grew hungrier. Once, he came home with his pay—about twenty dollars for the week. He started an argument with momma, as usual. As he spiraled deeper into his addiction, his frustations grew stronger. He had become increasingly unhappy. I've learned that addicts take the brunt of their anger out on those who are closest to them. "I'll show you, dammit," he said, and then threw the twenty dollars in the coal stove. We suffered greatly the following week. This episode led me to Mrs. Granger's house that day to ask for a sandwich for lunch. This was the most humiliating thing I've ever done in my life. I promised God that I would never do this again, even if I had to work four jobs. If black people are the most disenfranchised in society, the poor black person is the most unloved. If you're black and poor, you're at the bottom of the pile. Gloria was crushed when momma bought me a Schwinn bicycle for Christmas. I'll never understand that one either, but she did. It was stolen the first day that I rode it to Fairview Elementary School. Momma and

I both cried because we knew she denied my sisters so I could have that bike. Schwinns cost big bucks. At this point, I knew it just wasn't fair that I receive special treatment.

The older I became the harder I worked. I appreciate the work ethics my mother instilled in me during those early years. I finally figured out that momma was grooming me to be a source of support in the coming years. I was a good student and a respectful little boy. She taught me to smile and to always say yes ma'am and yes sir. I found that people liked good children and would do more for them than those who were disrespectful. I used what mama taught me to becoming a young con in the making. Not only was I a thinker, I was a good observer and found that the greatest show on earth is simply watching and observing people, I learned that from my daddy.

CHAPTER FIVE - DRUID CIRCLE

We moved to 1015 Druid Circle off of Statesville Ave. My daddy's drinking was very bad at this point. Every weekend, the police would bring him home in a station wagon or a hearse. They used any available vehicle back then to transport drunks home. Society's answer and solution to drunks back then was to embarrass them into sobriety. The people they hurt and embarrassed the most was their families.

They carried him like he was dead. I was getting older and it was so embarrassing. I guess today, knowing what I do about addiction, I should have been grateful that they brought him home instead of leaving him to lie in the streets. Much worse things could have happened to him he could have been run over and killed. I would often be playing baseball in the street with my friends when the hearse or station wagon drove up like clockwork every Friday. I would run and hide in the woods before the vehicle would stop at my house. I'd sometimes stay there for a while and cry because I was ashamed to go back and play with the other kids. Eventually, I'd go into the house through the back door. Daddy was laid out on the bed. He thought he never hurt a soul but himself. The mantra of people with substance abuse problems is this: "I ain't hurting nobody but me so just leave me alone." In truth, everyone who loves this person is hurt. Some carry emotional scars that never heal.

Like most people, I could not understand what compelled anyone to drink and drink, knowing the misery that always followed, to be powerless. This scenario today is what I call "dancing with the demon." Most people, even today feel that the afflicted person can simply stop if he were strong enough and had enough faith in God. I remember vowing to NEVER EVER be like my daddy. Little did I know that, one day, while I wouldn't reach the point of getting drunk and passing out, I would become exactly like him. Today, I'm actually proud of the fact that I inherited many of his traits and attributes. My aunt and uncle moved to Edison Street about three blocks from us. They didn't recognize us as family. When they rode by our house, they'd look the other way. Daddy tried to escape the shame of not being able to control his drinking and measuring up as a man by drinking more.

I had a different form of escape—stargazing. I enjoyed talking to God through His stars and planets. I thought that the universe was the most amazing creation that God had performed. It was always a thrill watching a shooting star and realizing that a meteor had died, and somewhere else another was being born. There was no greater escape than mentally being in space with the planets, the stars, the moon, and the meteorites. This was perfect peace. Everything was calm and serene. But reality was never far away. I'd look around to see that my dad was still a drunk. One day I was faced with the bitter fact that my momma had started drinking too.

She worked so hard and her family was still the lowest on the totem pole. She had begun to lose that wonderful sense of humor. She would come home from work and cry. I'm so damn tired of cleaning up behind white people, cleaning those damn commodes; I don't know what to do," she'd say between sobs. I noticed the neighbors next door who drank a lot also. I could literally see the increase in folk looking for the comforter. They were looking for something to ease the pain. That family was my first time ever witnessing spousal abuse. It wasn't the husband abusing the wife; she literally would beat the living hell out of him for no reason other than she was good and drunk. She was a visible example of people who take their frustrations out on those they love. She broke many a bottle over his head and anything else within reach.

When they were sober, all was well. They were good people who treated me the same as their children. I enjoyed being around them a lot. I just learned to duck when the drinking began. Even so, they were still what I had always wanted us to be, a loving, close family.

They took me to Cherokee NC with them once. That was one of the greatest thrills of my life. We saw the Cherokee Indians in their native garb. I thought about my daddy when I saw these kind and peaceful people. We saw the tepees and Mildred the Bear, who could easily drink fifty to sixty soft drinks a day. Mildred had a gut as big as Montana.

I had never been to the mountains, the beach or anywhere for that matter. I don't remember ever going anywhere with my daddy. The beauty of the Blue Ridge Mountains was awe inspiring, the trout streams, and the coolness of the air. The apples and other food were good all along the highway. There was honey, chow-chow, and pickled everything. Peanuts and pork rinds were either roasted or fried. There was also saltwater taffy. The ride up there and coming back was as much fun as when we got there. When I look back at my first grade photo, I realized why people like this family liked me. I had such an innocent little face. Things were changing at warp speed. The neighbor on the other side of us was the most beautiful wife I'd ever seen. She was a Godly woman. On a scale of one to ten, she was a twelve. Her husband was two different people when he drank. He would beat this woman on the sidewalk when he was drunk He would actually straddle her on the ground. Watching him showed me how people can change in an instant. I would scream from my yard to theirs, "Please don't do that; don't hit her again, Mr. John!""You'd better shut your damn mouth, boy, before I come and get you."

I was too frightened to say anything else. He had never cursed me before. He appeared to be a nice man when he wasn't drinking. I had never witnessed anything like this before. No one would help that poor woman. When he was through, she would go into the house and cry. I never saw these situations in Fairview Homes or Wyatt Street. This was one of my earliest recollections of how devastating addiction can be. When he wasn't drinking, Mr. John would call his wife sweetheart and treat her like a queen. But once the chemicals take control, that loving man was gone. I believe that all of a man's frustrations, disappointments, and anger surface when he's under the influence of any mind altering, mood changing substance. Why do people change like that I wondered? I would eventually find out from first hand experience. As the twig is bent the limb shall grow.

The older I became, the more I noticed drinking all around me. Addiction was progressing in our society. My family life worsened on a daily basis. My dad needed help. My mother was becoming so depressed that she was seriously talking of leaving my daddy. In the meantime, she continued to drink, looking for the comforter herself. We were sandwiched between neighbors who got drunk on the weekends trying to forget the treatment they endured during the week. How many times can a man be called "boy," and not want to punch that racist in the face? How much abuse a man take because he's trying to feed his family and not retaliate? The problem with weekend warriors is that need to escape ventured into Thursdays, then Wednesdays, and then to Monday until there were no more sober days. This is the domino effect of addiction. After a while, it consumes every waking hour.

As a person's dependency progresses so do the mood swings and violent tendencies. It gets to the point that the addict will do almost anything to get the substance that strengthens the addiction. I was five years old when I started school in the first grade, eleven years old when I left elementary for junior high, and thirteen in 1958 when momma received the call.

Chapter Six - Daddy's Life Changing Accident

"Oh, my God!" I heard her say. It was almost a whisper. I kwen something was wrong beacuse momma's eyes started welling up with tears "Your husband has been taken to the hospital," the caller had told her. He must have said something else because another "Oh my God," followed. This one was louder and fear became visible in her face. The police said that daddy had been struck by a car on North Graham Street around 5:20 PM. He was only six or seven blocks from Druid Circle. His leg was broken and his knee was in bad shape as well. When we got to see him, he was in a cast from the waist down. He stayed in the hospital for about two weeks and was sent home. From that day forward, he was unable to work. Now he was permanently on crutches and always at home.

Sometimes what we perceive as bad, God turns into good. What I do remember is that for the first time in my life, my daddy somehow, someway stopped drinking. Cold turkey. That was a miracle despite the fact that he was now crippled. His right leg somehow became shorter than his left. During those days Blacks received the most marginal medical attention. Little concern was given to a black person's quality of life. Bone fragments were left in daddy's knee that caused swelling and pain for the rest of his life. Although his leg hurt him badly during those years, he would take nothing more than a BC powder for the pain. He would not touch a drink. I thanked

God for the miracle. I had my father back and we began to talk about everything.

We talked for the first time about his career with The Three Stooges. He had traveled with them. He kept their outfits together and occasionally prepared their meals. I learned he'd worked at The Shubert Theater in New York City, and for wealthy families on Long Island. He had been a butler for the elite and the famous. He wore designer suits in the thirties. These were the greatest stories I had ever heard about my daddy. Those great stories about New York City would stick with me forever.

Daddy started eating dinner with us and becoming a part of the family. We actually talked as father and son. He began to smile and laugh again. One night daddy was scolding me about something and I was upset with him. Why I had this little penknife clinched in my hand I'll never know. When he saw it he thought that I had it for him and this really hurt my father. I'll never forget that incident. I meant to tell him for the longest how sorry I was that it happened but I never did.

Daddy became sullen and distant because of the toll on my mother as the sole breadwinner. He saw the burden it placed on her. To help out, I started carrying newspapers for Mr. Joe who lived across the street. This man was so smart he was a division manager with the Charlotte Observer as well as owning his own business. I was too young to work but he knew the situation at our home and bent the rules. He was one of the best examples of a loving husband and father that I have ever known.

I started my route in the summer and when the winter came, I fully understand what it meant to work at a job that takes more than it gives. That December was extremely cold. Sleet fell and a hard wind blew. My hands and feet were so cold I couldn't feel them. I had socks over my hands but they didn't stop the cold. When I got home, momma soaked my feet in cold water, "Hot water will hurt more," she explained. And because Mr. Joe believed in me, I went back the next day and did my job. He was a good man, and I did not want to disappoint him, or let momma down.

One of the biggest numbers man in Charlotte stayed down the street from us. Mr. T had two washing machines, one had dirty clothes in it; the other one was full of money. One of the hardest-working men in the neighborhood lived up on the corner. He was also self-employed cutting and selling wood. Mr. A was also a quiet man and a good provider. He took good care of his family. The difference between these two men and the drinkers we lived between was the fact they could take a nip on weekends and stop. They were always the same, no split personalities. They would never dream of abusing their loving wives. I always wondered why our family wasn't like them. Momma talked to us, but daddy remained distant. I became aware of how much fun everyone was having when they were drinking, especially at momma's fish fries. They were all whooping, and laughing at the top of their lungs. I liked seeing everyone having fun, walking into things, stumbling, and just acting the fool. After one of her fish fries, someone had left half of a drink. It was bourbon and coke. It smelled good so being devilish, I tasted it. It was strong at first, but then there was this incredible warm feeling in my stomach that spread all over. My head became light and I started to feel good instantly. After another sip, and another, there was "peace in the valley." I knew at that point why everyone was laughing and felt good. This was the beginning of my journey. I had met a new friend whose name was alcohol. I would become engaged to this friend and would spend years in the relationship.

Chapter Seven - Puberty

I finished the seventh grade. The eighth grade was nothing like elementary school but I did okay. I was no longer the smartest kid in the hood, or in my class. I had officially started seeing girls and dancing with them at the school dances and parties. The aroma of pot started to become more and more common. I remember the summer of ‘57 when I met Eric Summerfield. He and his family moved to Charlotte from Ohio. We took swimming lessons together and became friends. On the other hand, there was Bruce, who we called The Ghost because he was so pale and funny looking. Bruce was skinny and much older than we were. We would yell "ghost-ghost" and it was on. We were really afraid of this guy. eric and I became like brothers, we were close and had good times together getting into devilish things like yelling at Bruce from a safe distance and running until he gave out of breath and we did too. We'd sit on the playground stretched out laughing so hard we almost cried. However we never let our guard down because ole Bruce knew sometimes we were on the playground so we always had to keep a sharp lookout for the ghost.

Going to Northwest Junior High School in the fall of 1956, we walked to school across Double Oaks playground, walked the pipe over the creek, through the woods and then up Russell Street. The rules had changed from elementary school; peer pressure came into play. We had to be cool and hip to impress the girls. Boy, did these girls look cute and grown. Some of them really had points of their own. several years passed and I had begun to hang with the hipsters and tasted my first drink of wine after reaching the ninth grade. The older girl (K) from next door stopped by my house one day and told me to come over. She told me to come into the bedroom because she wanted to show me something. Being as dumb as cornbread, I believed her. She put her hands down my pants and grabbed me by the peanie. Immediately, I had an erection. She told me to take my pants down as she pulled down her panties. She told me to get on top of her and I did. She then inserted me into her. After a few minutes, I experienced my first ejaculation. I thought the bourbon and coke was great but WOW! I had never in my life felt this way before. It also scared me to death because I knew enough to know that this is how babies are made and I was way too young to be a daddy. I went home immediately and was too afraid to be around anyone for a while. But that fear passed and this event became a habit with her. As I became more interested in being cool, my grades started slipping fast I did so well on my paper route and getting the most new customers that I won a trip to the beach. I had never seen the ocean. I was so excited. Gene G. was from Charlotte and had won a trip too so we went together. It seemed to take forever to get to the beach but when we did and I saw all of that water, I was happier than I'd ever been. Gene and I bought some fireworks. We were having the time of our lives. Then one of us had a bright idea. We found some soft drink bottles and would light the firecrackers, put them in the bottles and run. This wouldn't have been so terrible except the bottled exploded all over the beach. All of a sudden, a big man came walking towards us very fast.

He shouted "What are you doing? Do you realize dat dis glass will be all ovah da beach? People will walk on it and cut dere feet. I'm the constable, and I'm going to lock you up!" We were terrified. He looked at us like a mad man with his very large eyes. He was as black as coal, and looked to weigh 300 pounds. He was furious and we were two scrawny scared little boys. He yelled at his partner, "Bring me de handcuffs." We began begging and pleading. Instead of handcuffs, his partner bought two rakes from the trunk of their police car. "Git started," he said. "Git every speck of glass or I will lock you both up." We were happy to rake. We would have raked a solid mile had he wanted us to. "That's one mean Geechie," Gene said. "What's a Geechie?" "Lawd, have mussy, this boy don't know nuthin. Lil bro, a Geechie is someone from Charleston. You ain't never been nowhere have you?" "Nope." I didn't care where he was from or who his parents were. I just knew that we never wanted to see that man again in this lifetime. After we finished, we went up to the outdoor dance floor and watched people dancing. The lights and music were incredible. The aroma of fish frying wafted through the air. People danced to the tunes of Fats Domino, Bobby Blu Bland, The Coasters, Hank Ballard, and Wilbur Harrison.

The next night, we were walking near the rides and heard this man shouting into a bullhorn, "Gitcha Hoochie Coochie Momma, watch her rock and roll if you can stand it. Hoochie Coochie momma, Gitcha Hoochie coochie." We witnessed our first hoochie coochie show and were embarrassed to see what we saw. This rather heavy woman rolled her hips and squatted in her very skimpy outfit. I could have sworn that the stage was actually leaning from side to side. I soon found out that it was. She invited people to come up and would put their hands between her legs. When she danced, the stage would rock and squeak. After a while, she invited everyone to come in and see the real deal. "Any real men out there?" she shouted. "If you want to come in, it'll only cost ya a quarter." We didn't go in. Frankly, I was scared. She wasn't good looking, and quite heavy. Some of the men were drunk and stumbling; we didn't know if a fight would break out or what. We had seen enough of the hoochie coochie momma. As we walked, I detected something more than fish frying. "What's that Gene", I asked? "Lawd, have mussy. You don't know what that is? Boy you just as country as you can be. That's reefer." "What's reefer?" He sighed and said "POT, DAMMIT, POT!" "What's pot?"

"JESUS CHRIST LAWD HAVE MUSSY, WHEW," he said, shaking his head. He just looked at me. "god dammit! If you don't ask me anymore questions, I'll buy you a cotton candy, okay? Okay? Just be quiet for the rest of the night." The rest of the night was the only reprieve he got because I started again the next morning. I hated to leave the beach; being there was the most fun that I had ever had anywhere. As we drove home, I saw Myrtle Beach from a distance. "Can we go down there?" Gene looked at me and there was a long pause... "No, we can't go down there," he said quietly "Why I asked? He looked up for along time, took a deep breath and said exercising all of his discipline cause we're colored." "Oh," I said, still not understanding, but I figured I'd give him a break. I wasn't going to ask any more questions he was tired and it showed in his face. I had worked him overtime.

Chapter Eight - The Boy Scouts, Violence and Carla

I joined the Boy Scouts at First Baptist Church on Mint Street. It was so much fun telling ghost stories at night around the campfire and scaring the bejesus out of the younger scouts. The scoutmaster's favorite story was about how our campsite was on top of an Indian burial ground and how their spirits would walk among us when we slept. There was always total silence during these stories and eyes as big as teacups. I realized how much I loved the outdoors and nature. After camp one summer, I met this guy named Pookie Garrett who lived down the street with his mother. Boy did we ever get into trouble together. One day, after leaving Pookie's house, I had walked about five blocks when I heard five loud gunshots. I followed the commotion and saw at least ten police cars. An officer was on the ground bleeding. A woman was nearby. Her face was totally distorted and bleeding profusely. "What happened?" I asked a nearby kid. "That cop was beating this old woman to death and her son took the bastard's gun from him and shot him five times!" he answered. I knew immediately to get the hell away from there. Other cops had surrounded the woman's son and were beating him mercilessly. I thought to myself, 'he should have killed the muthafucker. What would he have done if someone beat "his" mother like that?'

I saw the hatred in those cops eyes, and fear as well. I rode the bus home hating anything that had blue, gray, or green eyes. I knew that Elijah Muhammad was right about them being devils and began to understand exactly what that Malcolm X was talking about when it came to these evil people. Summer was over; it was time to go back to school. I was adjusting well and becoming more popular but my grades continued to slip. That year, I met Carla, this drop dead gorgeous girl from England. The boys and I were walking home from school. "Lawd, have mercy," I said. "Who is that? Boy, she's fine!" "Why don't you ask her?" someone asked. "He's too scared," another said. "Go and ask her with your scared ass." "Not me, I'm not scared of anything." "Then go!" I mustered up the courage, walked faster, caught up with her and felt as though I was going to faint. "Hi. Can I walk you home?" Her response was "we're walking, aren't we?"

With that British accent that wouldn't quit, this high yellow sister could knock the socks off any man. She was stunning. I carried her books and walked her to Double Oaks where she lived. I floated all the way home to Druid Circle, four blocks away. I was officially in love for the first time in my life. We talked and established a wonderful relationship that lasted a year or so. During those times, the love songs were out of this world. When Ann Murray sang "Snowbird" and Johnnie Mathis sang "Chances Are" I thought of nothing but Carla. She was beautiful, as was her entire family. She had a drop dead gorgeous mother and two sisters who were very pretty as well. These women had something that I was not accustomed to in friends and associates. They had class. The way they carried themselves, spoke, and behaved let me know they had been reared well by their highly dignified mother. They held their heads high, always spoke using proper enunciation and pronunciation. They also held eye contact.

I really don't remember what happened but I began establishing a pattern of running from intimacy and healthy relationships. Subconsciously, I was afraid of intimacy and it took me many years to get to the root cause of it. Sometimes I wondered if I wasn't afraid of succeeding not just in relationships but at life in general. Napoleon Hill states that, "whatever the mind can conceive and believe, it can achieve." If that were true, I had the major components for success. I was a dreamer, had the belief system, and was a good thinker. Even so, I began to notice the brief encounters I had with good people. Enduring relationships became a missing link in my life that would continue for many years to come. Nonetheless, I enjoyed the popularity and attention during these years. I could sing and knew it. I had started to mature physically. One music teacher, who was built like a brick house, liked me. I think she liked me a little too much. One day I had some type of rash on my arm and I was scratching. After class she told me "don't scratch for it, ask for it." I was dumbfounded. No, I never asked for it, I wish I had but it took me a while to figure that one out. I missed it completely still dumb as cornbread.

Chapter Nine - The Journey Begins

Gene was right about the reefer, at this party one night. Fat Daddy had it and things started going to new levels for me quickly. I realized that I had been missing what the adults already knew: Reefer made everything okay. The summer of 1959 brought new adventures with girls and drugs. I had met the best friend of my life for a long, long time. Sex started becoming more frequent and had lost all the innocence it once had. I was no longer the victim; I was becoming the conqueror. Even so, I was still a country pumpkin. Someone told me that if you put fertilizer on your face, your hair would grow. I tried for four weeks and finally gave up, nothing happened. I wanted a moustache and wanted to become a man quick.

I began working at the Commodore Yacht Club in South Carolina as a bus boy. I sometimes would ice the glasses for the bartender when he became busy. I watched the bartender closely as he mixed Rob Roys, Martinis, Whiskey Sours, Manhattans, and Tom Collins. I worked hard and would sometime receive tips simply because people liked me. I remember once when this white woman was pretty drunk, she tried her damnedest to get me into the bathroom. Under no circumstance was I going into ANY room with her; No No). Being caught in a bathroom with any White woman was literally a death wish. I was no fool; I knew the consequences. We'd heard about the lynchings and the brutal beatings of black men for simply looking at a white woman. If I had indulged in this sexcapade, the only thing that would be left of me today would be a marker and an epitaph.

One of the waiters who saw it all told me, "You're the biggest fool in the world. I would've worn that thing out." "That's because you haven't had your medication today," I said. "You must be crazy as hell." I worked there for the duration of the summer. Work was a joy because I was starting to feel better about working hard and helping my mother. There were perks at work as well; I was being rewarded with the little smiles when we were finished. That's what the bartender called it. I had found the comforter. My testosterone level was so high at that point that I was completely out of control. I was knocking down steel doors single handedly. I remember getting phone calls at sometimes 11:30 at night from my girlfriend, T. I'd sneak through the window while her parents and sister were asleep, and take care of business. Talk about insanity. Imagine walking across a pitch black playground at 11PM at night through deathly dark woods, and then another ten blocks for some wee wee.

Chapter Ten - "As the Twig is Bent so Grows the Tree"

I knew I had a good heart and loved people, but I was becoming more and more confused about life and myself. As irresponsible as I was, it's amazing that I didn't father thirty children. Today, I know that it's not just women who prostitute themselves recklessly, but men as well. I was only looking for love in all the wrong places. I was an unguided missile heading to a theater near your daughter. I salute and hold extreme respect for the single female parents. Some of them really perform miracles keeping their children in the fold and on course. Being fatherless or motherless isn't necessarily about the absent parent physically, but being mentally and spiritually vacant as well. There are millions of mothers and fathers who are addicted and still in the home. They are setting terrible examples with their behavior and mannerisms. They are setting examples of domestic violence and extreme profanity right in front of the children. In some cases the situation would actually be better if that parent left.

At this point, I was still giving momma all of my money, except for maybe five dollars a week. I also dated the bartender's daughter. In the fall of 1959, I stepped into a brand new world called High School. I was going to the most popular black school in the state. This was the home of the Lions, aka West Charlotte Senior High School. The people were bigger, more mature, and wow, the girls were prettier and more grown-up. Some of them had bodies by Fisher but some had minds by Mattel. My first year consisted of football, basketball games, and talent shows. I didn't play sports but buddy, we could sing big time. We boys used to sing in the bathroom and I was always the lead singer. The acoustics in that tile bathroom were incredible. The sounds would resonate from the walls and when we had good harmony, half the school was outside the window listening and screaming for more. We could really deal with the Drifters (On Broadway) the Coasters (Yakkity Yak-don't talk back), The Moonglows, The Flamingos, and the Dells. We sounded good and knew it. These were the days of Maurice Williams and The Zodiacs and their all time hit 'Little Darling,' and Chris Harris and the Delacardos.

We were in demand at the talent shows and once again, I needed protection because there was a lot of jealousy. Captain Snag, Peter R, and others were my adopted big brothers. These guys were all a lot older than me. They had already finished high school and were good football players. Keg Apple was a bad hombre who was always bullying little guys and those with no protection. I think he was bad because he had a complex about being short. He looked to be forty or older in high school. He had a large head and a face that could frighten Frankenstein. He made the mistake at a football game of telling me he was going to kick my ass after the game if I didn't give him a quarter. I told Peter and Captain Snag. "Walk through the gate," Snag said, "we got your back." Keg Apple didn't see them; he collared me. In a flash, Peter and Captain Snag tore him away from me and proceeded to wail on his dark ass, big time. He slid under the school bus for safety. They played soccer with him, kicking him from one side of the bus to the other about eight times. Keg realized there was no way out and begged my forgiveness. When he came from under that bus he couldn't stop saying, "Man, you know I wuz playing, tell Peter and Snagg I wuz playing."

We all laughed so hard that he finally did too, although nervously. He always wanted to buy me something from that day forward: a soda, popcorn, candy. I always accepted. I was such a smart kid and a good businessman as well. One thing I couldn't understand was how I could never have a lasting relationship like some of the other guys. Mine would last a few months or so and then it was over. I didn't realize it then but I was quite unstable. It seemed that I was never satisfied. It was funny but it seemed as though the more sex that was involved, the shorter the relationship lasted.

My drug use escalated. I only knew reefer and alcohol at this point, but that was about to change. Javan and I were classmates and we started to hang together. He told me about Big Alvin, one of the biggest bootleggers in Charlotte. He would have other people sell for him. He was a wholesale distributor. His white liquor came directly from the distillers (in the mountains.) He hired Jay and me as runners. He figured that no one would stop two kids walking with paper bags. We knew there was liquor in these jars. One day, Jay suggested that we take a swig. Soon, we were bow-legged drunk and barely delivered the package almost an hour late. We had a short career in the delivery business when big Al found out that we had been testing the product.

Our short career in crime was christened at the playground. Jay was not a good influence on me at all. The Queen City Classics Game was coming up. This was the biggest football game of the year between Second Ward and West Charlotte High Schools.

Walking home one day, Jay says, "Man we can make some money off of the tickets to the game." We had no money, so naturally, I asked, "How are we gonna get tickets to the game." "Take them. I know where they are," Jay said, "They're in this locker in Ms. G's room." "No no, not me buddy um um!" I said. "You're still scared as hell, aren't you?" "I'm not scared; I just don't want to go to jail." "Ain't nobody going to jail, they'll never know who took them." He worked on me all the way home and I finally agreed, like a fool, to go along with it. I was never more afraid in my life we went through the window at school, broke the lock on the locker and took the tickets. I realized that I had committed my first crime. I was scared to death every day at school, especially when they announced on the intercom that someone had broken into a locker and took these tickets. The pencil that I was holding started shaking like crazy in my hand. I could hardly breathe, I started hyperventilating. The teacher asked me what was wrong. I lied and told him I had asthma and that I'd be fine.

Jay had it all planned; he would give the tickets to Niecee, a sister from the hood who would hide them in her bra and sell them for us. Earl C, this fresh teacher who had a reputation for fondling girls just happened to fondle Niecee that day. She jumped, and the tickets fell from her bra. Geese were being prepared to be cooked. She sang big time. She sang in every octave she knew, she told not only on us, but everything other students had done too. I was terrified when they announced over the intercom for Thomas Saunders and Javan K to come to the office. Jay was a seasoned liar and denied everything. I was too nervous and scared to deny anything. Shaking like a leaf, I hung my head and admitted to it all. We were promptly suspended from school and told not to come back without our parents. Momma was furious and really wore me out with that belt. There was no joking or acting this time, momma really gave me a good ass whupping.

The next day, both our mothers came to school with us. Talk about too much TV, we wore black shirts and white ties to school because we thought at this point we were gangsters for having committed a crime. Mr. B didn't take to this too kindly at all. Momma told me to apologize, which I was very glad to do. Mr. B proceeded to wear our asses out with that very large paddle of his. We were or least I had an aching but for some time that day.

Chapter Eleven - The Gradual Descent and Racism

My grades were in the basement. I started hanging out more down at the Double Oaks Sundries. There was this guy named Johnnie D who was certainly one of the strangest kids that I had ever met. We called him Steel Head because he would run as fast as humanly possible, take a running leap, and crash his head into the trunks of cars. They opened every time. He even damaged the trunks. I never understood how he didn't suffer a concussion or fractured skull. No one ever bothered him because after all, he could kill with that head. One night, this carload of white boys came roaring through. They threw bottles and yelled, "nigger, nigger." We reciprocated by throwing bricks back at them, which was futile. We hardly ever saw whites because we lived in a period of segregation. The lunch counters would not serve colored people, period. When we shopped, a very cold "Whatcha need?" accompanied the constant glare of the salespeople. Their faces wore perpetual frowns. I never understood the hatred. We soon found out that my middle sister was pregnant. It's amazing how history repeats itself. Momma had my older sister in her teens. This represented a big change in the household. After all, we were adding a new member to be named Thomas Antoine. The father was a member of the Zodiacs Band. It was tough enough fending for ourselves. Now, there was another mouth to feed. He was such a beautiful baby.

I started seeing Joy that summer. Her dad was the headwaiter at the Charlotte City Club and I went to work there as a waiter. I was a good waiter and impressed the bartender by helping him when he was behind. I saw Charlotte's powerful and elite here at the Charlotte City Club. We wore red jackets, white shirts, and bowties. We were sharp as tacks. Joy's dad had a habit of snapping his fingers at us to impress the whites and to feel a sense of control and power as well. He could be as cold as ice and very demanding. He would fire you on the spot. He liked me because I was dating his daughter, whom he was crazy about. "If you ever fuck up or hurt her, I'll castrate ya!" he told me. He never had to tell me that again. It was a definitely a priority for me to have a good relationship with "his" daughter.

It seemed like every time I saw a good-looking woman, I fell in love. What I thought was being in love, I later learned was being in heat. The summer and fall came and went. I was beginning my senior year when I met Gin. She was a sophomore and we started a wonderful relationship. This relationship was different. I was a little more mature and we became real friends. She was younger, funny, unpretentious, and pretty. We saw a lot of each other. I totally enjoyed being around her because together, we were both funny and enjoyed each other's company. I was really attracted to Gin, and I think she cared for me as well. A lot of the attraction came from her sincerity and honesty. We lasted a full year or so. I was finally looking forward to graduation.

I don't know how I made it out of high school but I did. Claude D, Edward R, and I decided to do what all kids do when they finish high school; we went to the beach. On the way down to Carolina Beach, about 40 miles out of Wilmington, NC, we saw a billboard that had a white robed man on a horse and a hood over his head. The billboard read "Welcome to Klan Country." We almost turned around; we had never seen anything like this. We decided that we had driven over four hours and there was no way that we were going back to Charlotte. We weren't on the beach an hour before a deputy came over to us and told us that we needed to go to another area. He pointed us to the colored beach. Claude was pouting and indignantly asked him, "Why do we have to go there?" "Because I said so; that's why. Further more if one of these white women complains about you,

I'll have no choice but to lock all of you up."We grumbled, but we knew we were a long ways from home. This was Dare County, the home of the Klan. We didn't want to end up dead. We spent hours on the beach until it was time to head back to Charlotte.

God showed me a white saint (a good man)

On the way back to Charlotte, my Impala started making a racket like it was coming apart. It was late at night about 9:30 PM. The two-lane highway was pretty much abandoned and jet-black. There were no service stations, no stores, no nothing. I was driving. I didn't tell them but I was seriously scared. I really didn't have to because we were all scared to death, we were in Klan country, and it was pitch dark. At that moment, I saw something that could have easily been the face of God. There was a faint light in the distance. As I drove, it became lighter and the racket became louder. It appeared to be a roadside store with White men repairing a car. We were scared because we didn't know if they were klansmen or what but we had no choice but to approach them. We pulled into the little shop with a gas pump outside. There is no doubt that they looked at us and had pity. "Your converter's come loose son he said". It might have lasted another ten miles or so and you would have been stranded," one of them said. All three of us had a grand total of $20.00 between us. Nervously I asked him, "How much will it cost?" "More than you've got, son." I dropped my head and absolutely didn't know what to do. I figured we would sleep in the car and pray for a miracle. The miracle came very early, the same man told me before I could get back into the car to pull the car into the stall and that we could sit on some benches out side.

"All we have is twenty dollars" I said. Pull ya car in here, son," he said. "Thank you, Lord," I said under my breath, "Thank you." About two hours later, I collected money from Claude and Edward, and along with mine, reached it out to him. I must have thanked him a dozen times. I'll never forget what he said to me. "Son, how in the Sam Hill do you think y'all gone git home? You've only got a quarter tank of gas; keep that money." He told us to pull up to this 1894-looking gas pump. I thought that it was just an antique but he cranked that baby up and filled the tank. I will never ever forget that white man—that good white man who may have been an angel in disguise. He literally saved us from who knows what. I learned a very valuable lesson that day. I learned that people are just people. I also learned that "there's some bad in the best of us, and some good in the worst of us so it doesn't behoove any of us to talk about the rest of us." (big book) This is so true. We drove back to Charlotte thanking God every ten minutes. We did that unabashedly back in those days because we could've been in big trouble. We could have been stopped on any stretch of that highway and all of the residents could have been Klan.

Chapter Eleven - Johnson C Smith University (a brief encounter)

Momma had convinced me to attend Johnson C. Smith University. She was working there as a maid. I lasted every bit of three months because I simply could not focus on anything related to my studies. I didn't know what was happening to me. At one time, I had been destined for the accolades of Magna Cum Laude. But that was then, this is now. Homework had become alien; I didn't even try. I had changed so much from the kid in grade school who made straight A's to flunking out of college. I made a decision to beat them to the punch and quit. I was becoming a quitter at everything. I ran from anything that was challenging or what I perceived to be a problem. Low and behold, I had another bright idea. I would move to New York City. I was a top-notch bartender and waiter; why not? I spent another year in Charlotte working as a waiter and doing nothing. I met Mary Y, who was older than me. This time my sexcapades produced a baby girl. I was afraid and happy at the same time.

It seemed that I already lived two lives. I was only eighteen years of age, and in eight months, I would be a father. I could see that I had no self-control. I simply had to become more responsible. I couldn't blame anyone for my actions—not momma nor daddy. I was the one responsible. Oh sure, I could say that my daddy wasn't there for me and that our family was totally dysfunctional, but hey, they all are.

Eight months passed and there she was, Renee. She was such a beautiful baby. I was so out of control that Mary told me after a night together a few weeks later that she was pregnant again. I remember the exact night that it happened. I was lit and pretty much forced her against her will to have sex with me. Our new baby wasn't even a month old. I've always wanted to do the right thing but my flesh was very weak; I was standing on very shaky ground. About eight and a half months later, there was another beautiful baby girl. I was about as ready to be a father as an orangutan was to perform a lobotomy. Mary was a very good mother. I did the absolute best that I was capable of doing as a nineteen-year-old kid with two baby girls. When Renee was a year old and Regina was two months old, I received the shock of my life. I called one day and was informed that Mary had simply left. "Where is she?" "I don't know," was the response. "You don't know?! What do you mean you don't know? Where are the babies?" "She's gone and the babies are with her, Thomas. Please don't ask me anything else."

I figured that she was upset with me about something and was in Rock Hill with her relatives. She'll be back in a couple of days, I hoped. She didn't come back in a couple of days, weeks, or months. I didn't have a clue where she and the babies were. Little did I know that it would be over twenty years before this question would be answered. I didn't know what to feel, I was used to playing with the babies, and now they were gone. I had no idea where to start looking because none of her relatives would tell me anything. I missed the girls very much, they were as cute as they come. This separation caused major problems later in life. My dependence on mood altering chemicals progressed. After twenty years, when Mary returned to Charlotte, I learned that she had taken the babies to Detroit. Today I know how cruel and unfair this was to me. But when I had a moment of clarity, I also knew she was right. I wasn't prepared to be a father. I couldn't even be responsible for me. She thought that she was doing what was best for her and the babies. Soon afterwards, I met Carolyn. She was to become my wife at a future date. She was also a party girl who drank. I found out that water seeks it's own level, so do people. We were attracted to each other because of similar backgrounds. She went to Second Ward and was a year ahead of me and older as well. She moved to Washington DC to live with relatives and I was preparing to go to New York City. During my junior year in High School, I had bought a 1960 Chevrolet Impala convertible that was black. It was one bad boy. I kept that baby as clean as a maternity ward and was anxious to put that baby on the road.

Chapter Twelve - New York City

Edward R, Touta, a female friend, Mitch L, and I headed to New York City via Washington, DC. Mitch and Touta were getting off in DC. After arriving in Washington, we smoked pot in the car. I was a little turned around and guess what? Because pot makes you so bright, I looked for a policeman to give us directions. Finally, I saw one. I was about to roll down the window when everyone yelled, "Don't open the window; don't open the window!" The cop had rolled his window down. I was petrified and had to think of something quick. I cracked the window about a centimeter and acted as though I knew exactly where I was. "I got it officer; I know where it is," and off I went. I just knew that it was a matter of time before the policeman would turn his vehicle around and the familiar sound of the siren would be behind us. We ended up on Benning Road. I never heard the end of that. I hadn't realized until then how stupid people become after using pot. It's almost like walking into the Police Station and offering them a joint. I dropped my passengers at their designated places in DC and headed towards New York City. We were going to stay a while with Edward's mother until we got our own wings. We drove and drove and drove. It really didn't seem that long because the traffic on the Baltimore-Washington, the Delaware, and the New Jersey Turnpikes was fast traffic.

Finally, we came to the Rahway, New Jersey exit and there it was. We saw the biggest and most magnificent city in the world. We went through the Holland Tunnel, and when we came out...Wow. There were people everywhere, lights everywhere, and car horns that blew from every direction. I was so excited that I had only my park lights on going the wrong way down a one-way street. All of a sudden, we were motioned to pull over by a traffic cop. I was trembling at this point. I though that we were going to jail. The cop knew that we were young and dumb. "Turn on your lights." He was friendly. "How do I get to Harlem?" We were going to 123rd Street. That's where Edward's mother lived. I don't know till this day how I negotiated driving up the Westside Highway. I was absolutely awed by the spectacle of New York City. I had never in my life seen anything so bright, big, and endless. The sounds of New York City were like a symphony, a real life concert. It took a while to drive over 115 streets but we were rolling. When we finally reached 125th, we took a right and drove towards Lenox Avenue. Man, was this ever something. We had beautiful girls in Charlotte but man, oh man!

All of the rules changed in New York City and things went to another level. These were the real players and drop-dead foxes. I fell in love six times in six blocks. These women were built for pleasure, I almost ran up on the sidewalk three times. They were holding and knew it. I saw the Famed Apollo Theater, Small's Paradise, and all of the hangouts that I had seen on TV. I couldn't sleep that night because of all the excitement. The show never stopped, it went on all night. This was the weekend, and the City was jumping. We reached Edward's mother's place and found a place to park. I wanted to walk back to 125th Street. I'm sure everyone knew that I was a tourist because I was walking and turning around as I walked.

That Sunday, we went to Central Park. This was a show in itself. I saw the Jewish Families, the Japanese, the Africans, the Puerto Ricans. Central Park was the greatest show on earth. We spent the day ogling women. I couldn't wait to see Monday morning because I had a date on Park Avenue at the office of Mr. S. I called him at 8:30 AM Monday. His mother had already called him to expect me. He gave me specific instructions on how to get to his office. I rode the train with all of these people. The subway was an experience in itself. Some of the characters looked so cold and distant. Edward's mother schooled me well: never look a stranger in the eye for any reason in New York City.

I climbed the subway stairs to Park Avenue. A different world awaited me. The people were dressed to kill and were very professional. They carried briefcases, even the women, but no one ever spoke to anyone. I'm sure they knew I was country because I was speaking to everyone. Some of the women smiled but never spoke. I found 1420 Park Ave and went inside. There was brass and glass everywhere. It looked like money, smelled like money, and was money beyond the shadow of a doubt. I took the elevator to the 44th floor of this glass tower and found his suite. A classy receptionist greeted me with, "Hello, how are you?" "Fine, I'm fine." I said and so was she. Good God almightyI said to myself under my breath. I fell in love again. It was none of that "Whatcha need" back-home treatment I was accustomed to from white folk. "I'm here to see Mr. S." "Ah, yes, he's expecting you Mr. Saunders. He'll be with you shortly. Please have a seat." I couldn't believe how everyone pronounced my name correctly. They would say Saunders like saun-a. Not Sanders, the lazy way that Southerners would always screw it up. Everyone spoke so cool and proper. I was nineteen years old, and this was the first time that anyone especially a white woman had called me mister.

Then comes Mr. S with a warm smile. He greets me, "Hi Tom, please come in. You've got a good handshake there." Thank you. I had learned a long time ago that a good firm handshake is a sign of a man's character and integrity. "What do your friends call you Tom, or Tommy?" Tommy sounded so cool so I responded, "Tommy, they call me Tommy." No one had ever told me, 'please' before. This was a good feeling. He offered me hot chocolate, coffee, and Danish rolls. I knew better than to refuse him "anything." I was hungry and tried not to wolf everything down too fast. He really made me feel at home in his office. I understood why they made the money they did. It was because of their professionalism, they knew how to deal with people. He made small talk for a while and then he proceeded to business. In his eyes, I was still a kid and he was right. He instructed me to report to this office that was hiring on 48th Street the next day. I was told that the line could be as long as six blocks. "Don't get into the line, Tommy," he said. "Go directly through the door; ask for Mr. Feinstein. He was so right about the line. It went on it seems to New Jersey. Boy, did I ever get some dirty looks from the people in line.

"Hey kid, where the hell do you think you're going?" "Who the hell does he think he is?" shouted this very large woman. I knew better than to look back. These were some rough looking characters. I was processed in twenty minutes, got my ID badge, and told to report to the Festival Of Gas on the Avenue of Commerce the next day. Man, did I ever feel like a big shot. It felt good to be treated as I was. That would have never happened in Charlotte. I actually bypass everyone and walked right through the door like a celebrity. I took the train to Flushing Meadows. Shea Stadium was being constructed so I could simply walk through to get to the Fair. I found the Avenue of Commerce and finally arrived at the Festival of Gas. I would ask for a Mr. Gaston (pronounced Gas-stone). He was French. I was taken on a tour of this incredible restaurant. He gave me a quick orientation and told me what time to be back in the morning. This place was as clean as the Board of Health. I walked around the Fair for a while and marveled at the size of it all.

When I did get back home it was around 5:30 and time for Edward to get home as well. I immediately told him that we were going to celebrate that night by going to Coney Island. I had never been to Brooklyn before and we got lost. We were going toward Long Island on the BQE before we were corrected and came back to Coney Island. Talk about eccentric, it was summer and these older Jewish women were wearing fur coats and walking through the streets. It was evident that these people had money and plenty of it. We had a wonderful time riding the wild mouse, the Cyclone, the parachute and eating those dirty Coney Island hot dogs. They were so good. We were having fun like never before.

People were totally different here in New York. It was so cool. There were real family units here and it seemed the blatant racism shown in the South didn't exist. People knew that we were country; it showed. My favorite hangout was the African Pavilion where I would see Miriam Makeba and Hugh Masekela. It was exciting. Over time, I lost being a country bumpkin. I didn't have a southern accent; I was cool and blended in well. As far as I was concerned, I was a New Yorker.

Edward worked for a laundry and dry cleaning service that delivered linen to the fancy hotels every day. One day he was so excited, he came through the door and shouted, "Guess who I saw today? Elizabeth Taylor and Richard Burton at the Waldorf Astoria." I would find that it was a common occurrence to see the rich and famous in the city so nice that they named it twice.

We always walk the famed 125th Street at night to watch the greatest show on earth. Some of the behaviors were hilarious, but sometimes it was tragic. Edward witnessed a man stab a woman to death in the street on 123rd. She was stabbed at least thirty times. I was grateful that I hadn't seen it. This type of trauma lasts a lifetime, and definitely requires counseling; it haunts you. I could only imagine seeing someone so brutally murdered.

Malcolm X and the Nation of Islam

One particular day, this articulate, tall, slim man was giving a speech somewhere on the corner of 128th Street and Lenox Avenue. this guy was full of fire and enthusiasm. "Who is that?" I asked a brother beside me. "Man that's Malcolm X. He's the man." With eloquence and power I had not known in a black man before, he spoke about the evils of racism and white people being devils. I found myself attending more and more of his speeches. This man never had a script, or anything written to speak from. He spoke from sheer knowledge. I was astounded. I was leaning more and more towards this belief of Black unity and black power. I had heard some of the brothers talking about a day in 1960 when a cop was shot five times in this Mosque and why he was killed. The Muslims didn't allow any law enforcement to enter their Mosque for any reason and apparently this one thought he could. He paid the price for his decision. I remembered how those southern cracker cops would stop Blacks and shine their flashlight straight into their faces, attempting to agitate them. They were looking for "any" reason to beat and take out their frustrations on a Black man. I had seen the beatings of Blacks on TV and heard the news reports of Blacks being routinely shot for pleasure. I knew how brutal and viciously we had been treated during the entire history of this country and how nothing seemed to have changed. We were so defenseless and unable to protect our women, mothers, fathers, and children from these racist and evil people.

Malcolm talked about self-respect and self-sufficiency. He told the people, "If you think they'll change one day and become human, then you're a fool… If you think they're members of God's family, look at the photo of the demons lynching some poor innocent Black; their children and wives smiling with glee." He especially talked about black on black violence and how this was a part of the racist plan to destroy every black person in America. He said that it was all a part of the racist master plan of dividing and conquering. I began going to the Mosque often to hear the message of unity, love, and respect for ourselves and each other. This man was full of fire and confidence. He represented the Nation of Islam and the honorable Elijah Muhammad. He could literally look into your soul. I even saw this man known as Louis 5 X later to become minister Louis Farrakan. The Muslims believed in righteous living and abided by a strict code of ethics and conduct in their relationships, marriages and dealings with people in general. I admired and respected them. Their food was healthy and the best that I had tasted since the Menonite restaurants in South Carolina. I've never tasted fried whiting such as theirs and the bean pies were wicked. I thought that I was going to become addicted to those glorious bean pies. I had never tasted anything that good in my life. These babies topped even the lemonade that the sisters made back in the days in the Fairview Homes.

The women and young girls looked so pure and clean. The thing that was most astonishing was the fact that none of them had any make up on. Their skin and entire countenance was glowing and fragrant. That ebony bronzed skin was more priceless than the hope Diamond. These women were so natural and feminine. My first statement when I saw these sisters was, "GOOD GAWD A MIGHTY. Where in the name of God did they come from?" These women were more beautiful than anything I'd ever seen in my life. They were so respectful and, to my disappointment, would not return my flirtations. I would wink until my eye developed a cramp. They would only smile and blush. I would walk five blocks out of the way some days just to speak to them. I learned the Arabic greeting of "Assalamu alakim, my sister." They would respond "Alakum salaam, sir." I didn't want any of them to call me sir. I wanted them to say, "Hi sweetie, baby, sweetheart or darling. I wanted to get married immediately, have triplets in a few months, and live happily ever after.

The Muslims were fearless, and about the only Blacks that would stand up for themselves and command the respect of people and the police. I had never seen this type of total respect for one another and themselves. Because I was determined to marry one of these beautiful sisters, I almost became a fixture at the mosque. I practiced everyday with this one sister. One day she gave me this wonderful smile and I figured it was on like a neckbone. However, it never went beyond that smile to my dismay. I really wnted to marry at least four of them The times back in those days were for the most part, good times. I saw a lot of misery and crime as I traveled around the city. I saw garbage that was unprecedented, rats that were big enough to vote, and total neglect by the City of New York. I never saw this neglect in midtown, or downtown for that matter. It seemed to be concentrated in parts of Brooklyn, Harlem, the Bronx, and Queens. Where the poor were, so was the garbage.

The Reality of New York City

I saw so many celebrities and performers on the streets. I remember seeing Adam Clayton Powell, and the day that Billy Eckstein was abducted from a street in Harlem. I think that it was 125th Street near Lenox Avenue. I saw Cassius Clay in front of the Hotel Theresa talking to King Curtis, the saxophonist. This was before he came Muhammad Ali, the greatest. Harlem was full of surprises. I remember seeing Rudy Lewis, the lead singer for the Drifters in front of the same Hotel Theresa. A few days later he would be carried out on a stretcher dead from a drug overdose. I began seeing, once again, the devastating effects of addiction. I also saw the direct correlation between drugs, poor health issues, and crime. A junkie would kill for a fix. Drugs explained prostitution. A high percentage of all prostitutes the world over are addicted. They will do anything for a few dollars more to get a fix. "I'll never become like that," I swore, not realizing my dependency was growing. Each day when Edward and I got off, we would go cruising. I loved getting lost learning my way around. One day we wound up in Rome, New York—a long way from home; seriously lost. We'd smoked some hashish and a couple of joints. We took "many" wrong turns. It really didn't matter; we were having a good time just driving and singing "na na na na na late at night, I count the tears…" was one of my favorites by the Drifters.

Foolishly, I stopped. "Again," high as hell, of all the people in Rome, New York, who did I ask for directions? You guessed it, a traffic cop. He asked me, "Son, how in the hell did you manage to wind up here in Rome?" I assured him that it was easy. Even he had to laugh on that one. It took quite a drive to get back to the City and the Triborough Bridge. I had relatives in Hempstead out on Long Island. One day we were cruising in Queens when we saw these two cute Italian girls. I yelled, "Hey baby, wanna ride? To my astonishment, she sweetly asked, "Do you have any gas, baby?" "Sure do," I said thinking that it was on and that I definitely was hot stuff until she then said softly: "You do? Then she yelled STEP ON IT CHUMP!" My feelings were really hurt for a minute. I was embarrassed, but we were just having fun. We drove out to Long Island to see my great Aunt Eunice. My sister is named for her. She had a nice home. Rita, my cousin, and her two children lived with her. Talk about the aristocrats in the family, they were all of that. Aunt Eunice was simply amazed. "Clyde Junior, you don't sound southern at all."

It was always embarrassing to hear some of the folk back home sound so ignorant with their speech. "I never have," I assured her. I went on to tell her that I worked at The World's Fair and lived in Manhattan, proud of myself. She was so pleasant to be around. She then did something that Northerners are not famous for. She said, "I know you're hungry Junior, let me prepare you some food." "OK," I said. Thank you, Lord. I was almost weak from hunger. I hadn't eaten all day. She prepared Edward and me the best, and tiniest sweet Italian sausage that I had ever had. I'd never heard of or tasted Italian sausages. She also gave us a teeny weenie spoonful of potato salad. I tried to take the smallest bites possible and to eat slower than I've ever eaten before. I was hungrier after I finished than when I began. Afterwards, she asked, "Would you like more?" "Oh no, I'm so full," I lied. I was getting weaker by the moment from hunger. I knew that Edward and I would stop at the closest Chinese or pizza joint and load up on the way back. I loved seeing all of the pictures on the wall of her, Rita, and the children. They were all so high yellow they actually looked white. I started to feel that somewhere in the past, my father was from a very distinguished tribe. Aunt Eunice's hair was flowing and snow white.

In New York City, if you take the wrong exit, make the wrong turn, you could easily wind up in Connecticut, or New England. Somehow, someway I took a wrong turn and drove for an hour in the wrong direction. All of a sudden, there was a tollbooth. The attendant asked, "What part of New England are you going to?" "NEW ENGLAND? WHAT? No way," I said. We told him we were trying to get back to Manhattan. He laughed knowing we were lost and told us, "Thank God for this toll, otherwise you'd be driving twenty-five more miles before you could turn around." He gave us directions, let us turn around, and we were on our way. It was getting dark and there was no way that I was stopping for anything before we were on 123rd Street. We finally arrived and found a parking spot. We walked up the stairs through a thick cloud of marijuana. Chico, one of the neighbors, was sitting in the midst and offered me a toke. "Que pasa, amigo?" I said. I took a long hit and kept going up the stairs.

I loved everything about this incredible city, the pizza, the franks, the bagels, the people, the horrendous traffic, the cabbies honking their horns, Central Park, Coney Island even the smell. On my days off, I would hang out in Greenwich Village or Washington Square, known as Needle Park, so named because the junkies would discard their works anywhere. I knew better than to ever take my shoes off there. I really enjoyed talking to the older people about anything, I learned a lot. For some reason, it always bothered me to see the homeless on the streets here just as it did when I was a child. It bothered me, but didn't seem to affect anyone else. It was almost like they were invisible to everyone else. Sometimes I would spend time in the Bowery talking to the homeless. I found out later that these people were engineers, surgeons, architects, lawyers, and everything else in the book. They had just taken a fall and needed help getting back on their feet. People always called them bums. Nothing could be further from the truth. It's true that in most cases drugs were a major reason for their fall, but I knew beyond the shadow of a doubt that they could be productive again. Society's answer for them was simple, "Keep moving. You can't sit there-if I see you again, I'm going to have you locked up." I realized over time how much I loved people and when they hurt, I hurt too. Occasionally, I would pick up a few sandwiches for my friends and have the deli worker to cut each one three ways. It wasn't much, but I saw that at least some of them ate. I could only imagine how they survived on those brutally cold New York nights. I knew one thing for sure and that was one of the reasons they drank so much wine was to keep from freezing to death.

"Seeing firsthand the problem and the shame associated with it."

After work the next day, I felt like walking up the prestigious Fifth Avenue. I met Antoinette, this very intelligent, good-looking sister from Queens. The way that I met women was simple. I was always lost asking for directions and would tell them I was from the South. They really thought I was lost and needed help. This usually started the conversation. Then I would admit that I knew exactly where I was and just wanted to meet them. This always produced a laugh or smile. Antoinette gave me her phone number. I invited her out immediately. We hit it off right away and she invited me over for a cookout. Everything was going fine until she offered me a drink of Tequila Sunrise. I probably had about three. They tasted great, only trouble was I didn't know when to stop. I actually fell asleep on her sofa, drunk, and she became mad as hell. She lived upstairs and she actually pushed me down the stairs. It was by God's grace and mercy that I didn't suffer serious injury. My feelings were hurt more than anything else and I immediately left going back to Manhattan—shamed and embarrassed. I'll never until this day know how I negotiated the Parkways and Freeways going back to the Triborough Bridge. There absolutely had to be a higher power that carried me back. I was as high as a supersonic jet. I had never in my life been drunk before and gone to sleep, except when Jay and I drank big Al's white liquor on the playground. I have no idea as to how I parked that baby.

I learned long ago that sometimes rejection from others can be protection from God. I would have been miserable in that relationship and so would she. That woman had a very cold heart, a very pretty face but a heart as cold as ice. Maybe her father was an alcoholic or she had been in an abusive relationship. She may have been a good person deep inside who had had a bad experience with someone. We talked the next day; she apologized for her actions. I assured her that I deserved it. I was upset with me as well. We saw each other a few times after that. I realized that there was something going on with Antoinette that she was not willing to share. The truth about the matter is there was a lot going on with ME that I wasn't willing to share either. Although we drifted apart, I really liked Antoinette a lot she was drop dead beautiful. I have learned the absolute necessity of honesty in a relationship, especially with yourself. I promised myself that I would never drink more than one drink from that day forward. That pledge lasted all of one day.

Chapter Thirteen - New York City-The Good Times

I started spending more time up on the roof. Smoking, drinking, and being alone with my thoughts. I could relate with Rudy of the Drifters when he sang "Up on the roof." "When this old world starts getting me down, and people are just too much for me to face… I'll climb way up to the top of the stairs and all my cares just drift right into space... On the roof, it's peaceful as can be and there the world below don't bother me, no, no So when I come home feeling tired and beat I'll go up where the air is fresh and sweet, I'll get far away from the hustling crowd and all the rat-race noise down in the street…" I wasn't sad or anything…or maybe I was sad and wouldn't admit it. I would think about my mom and dad and wonder how they were doing. I called about twice a month to check on everyone actually hoping on ocassion that someone would call and check on me.

Burrell J, one of my homeboys, was up visiting his two sisters, Ann and Sarah. I started hanging out occasionally with these two. Ann taught me how to roll a joint in the backseat of cars or taxis on even the roughest streets. She was a master. She was dating Art Blakey of the Jazz Messengers group. I was meeting people and learning new tricks everyday. I never had a problem fitting in because I liked people and what comes from the heart touches the heart. I really thought that I was living the good life. My tolerance to liquor was building. After staying with Edward's mother for some months, it was time to move on. We moved to Lenox Terrace on a 137th Street. Lenox Terrace today is a slum unless they've restored it. I really enjoyed going to Greenwich Village and hearing the jazz musicians. I loved Nina Simone, Thelonius Monk, Cannonball Adderly, and Rashan Roland Kirk. Brubeck was alive and well during those days as was Gerry Mulligan and Stan Getz. Remember that I was a jazz fan from the age of fourteen. I would drive to the Village because I could lose myself, and the hippies were always friendly people. Greenwich Village was so laid back; everybody was so cool. The people were very friendly probably because they were high as hell. These were the days of flower power. And the most powerful of all was the poppy. It was fashionable to carry Chianti around in the straw basket cover.

I started spending time in Washington Square when the hungry artists showed their work. There were a thousand shows a day in New York City and they were all free. Simply find a corner, any corner, and watch the people and the things they do. I then met Juanita, this very hot Puerto Rican girl who literally ran me down on Lennox Avenue. There was nothing shy about this girl. I was walking down Lennox Avenue and suddenly she was by my side asking, "Hey baby, where ya going? You kinda cute… wanna have some fun?" "Okay," I said. She was maybe two years younger and very street savvy. She lived on 10th Street and Lexington Avenue, in the heart of Spanish Harlem. This area was definitely more dangerous than Harlem. The Police answered calls there in mass. I never thought that Harlem was that dangerous. Spanish Harlem was home to some of the most notorious Latin gangs in New York City. She had a brother who was big and definitely a very bad hombre. When she introduced us, he showed me their handshake and their sign. He also showed me his tattoo that read "I will kill you before God gets the news." Before Juanita and I left, he looked me dead in the eye and said, "You ever hurt Juanita, I will find you quicker than the FBI and I'll bury you alive." I knew he meant it beyond the shadow of a doubt. He knew he had my attention. He followed that up with, "If you ever have any trouble, mention the name Houlio."

He never smiled but it got to the point that he trusted me. This particular night Juanita and I were cruising the Westside Highway going up towards Fort Apache the Bronx to visit some friends of hers. On the way back she suggested that we go to this spot and park. She immediately jumped into the back seat with me in tow. She pulled me on top of her and it was on. "Ooooh baby," she said. "God sho nuff didn't short change you, baby, He bless you wellll." The way that car was rocking, I was scared to death. New York City had legions of cops everywhere. In bed that night, I thought about things and started to realize that I was never satisfied. Little did I know that this was a part of my addictive personality. I always wanted to meet someone prettier, more intelligent, more articulate. The problem was and has always been "me" and some type of fear. I had no idea what I was afraid of, but I seemed to always be running when there was no one after me and there was no where to go. I was becoming very concerned about this relationship. I had always heard you should never cross a Puerto Rican woman. The results could be very hazardous to your health. One day Houlio came home and Juanita and I were engaging in serious business. He busted through that door like the terminator; they never knock unless the door is locked. I was scared to death and before I even had a chance to think I jumped from the first floor window. I was so afraid that I had forgotten how high the first floor was from the street. I was doing all I could to get my pants up. I hit the sidewalk and rolled into the street. I was in such pain, my ankle felt as though it was broken.

They laughed until she realized that I couldn't walk and was in very serious pain. Some of the locals pulled me up on the sidewalk because they'll definitely run over you in New York City. My ankle hurt so bad that I had to muster up all of my strength not to cry. You DON'T CRY for any reason in New York City. They rushed me to the Hospital on East 122nd Street. By the grace of God, I hadn't broken it. Houlio and Juanita drove me back home in my car, parked it, and took the train back to Lexington Ave. I was on crutches for over two weeks and had to take off from work. Anyone else would probably have been fired, but as they say, "It's not what you know, but who you know." Juanita came over daily. She'd be undressed by the time the door closed. She was definitely in charge; believe me. She told me, "If you ever cut out on me, I'll cut you a thousand ways from Sunday." I believed her. She was becoming a nuisance and wasn't too clean either. I had no idea what to do but I knew for a fact that I wasn't going to make her angry. The Latinos recognized no boundaries in warfare and I knew for a fact that Houlio was not a comedian. They will cross state lines for someone they want or who had crossed them. Today, Tiger Woods is such a phenomenon, little kids try to emulate him, dress like him; they even have their own little golf clubs. They look so cute walking through the neighborhood. Back then, if you saw a brother with teeth missing, stitches in his face, the look of a murderer on his face, and had a ragged golf club, he wasn't being cute. He was looking for somebody.

My younger sister Eunice was graduating from High School that year, 1964, and wanted to come to New York City to spend some time with her big brother. I made the arrangements with Aunt Eunice and it was on. I picked her and Margaret, a friend of hers, up from Grand Central Station. They were amazed at all of the people, lights, and the endless traffic. Driving back on the Westside Highway, I drove like all New Yorkers do, at breakneck speed. Eunice was so terrified and afraid of my driving that she ducked down almost to the floor to hide. I told her, "Sis, you're in New York City now. You'll get run over driving 45 miles an hour here." The next day I took them on a tour of the city and that night we went to the Apollo Theater. We saw Smoky Robinson and the Miracles, BB King, the Temptations after the show. All the entertainers would go to Small's Paradise after the show was over. We went there too. Eunice blurted out, "Lil bro, lil bro, ain't that Smoky Robinson and the Miracles?""Yep, sure is I told her. This is New York City, nothing like it anywhere in the world." Margaret was dying to try a martini. "Be careful," I cautioned her, "That's a strong one." "I can handle it," she said. I'm glad she thought so, I knew better. I wouldn't try more than two martinis myself. I ordered a small glass of wine for sis. Margaret had a second martini and was officially through. She almost passed out and was holding on for dear life. We all laughed.

We went next door to this $1.39 Steak House. The meat was tough enough to make shoes. They must have tenderized that cow for a week just to make it chewable. It was about 2 AM and I knew the girls were done. I was pretty tired myself so driving them back to Long Island would have to be at jet speed. Eunice was so terrified this time that she started crying. "Don't worry, Eunice," said Edward, "Thomas is a good driver, he knows what he's doing." In hindsight, I wished that were true about so many other things.

One night, we were sitting on the steps of our Brownstone when I saw a man who seemed to be a walking contortionist. He stood in front of us and bent over backwards and stayed in that position for what seemed to be an eternity. I wondered how in the world anyone could do that without breaking their spine. He looked like a paper clip. "What's wrong with that brother?" I asked one of the neighbors. "That's a junkie. He's high on hoss." I wasn't going to sound dumb again by asking him what hoss was. Edward whispered in my ear, "That's heroin." The time would come that I just had to check this Heh-ron out, as it was pronounced on the street. After witnessing this on a more frequent basis, I smoked some on some aluminum foil one night. Good God A Mighty, Whew! "Everything is beautiful," as the song says. I had never experienced anything like this before. I felt hipper, cooler, and so relaxed. I had now joined the major leagues. It was almost like having three orgasms at one time. I didn't develop an addiction immediately; it was very gradual. Matter of fact, I pretty much stuck with good pot and scotch. This worked well for me. Besides, I was afraid of Heh-run. I didn't ever want it to make me become a contortionist. I made the mistake of telling Juanita that my sister and her friend were in New York. She wasted no time in meeting her future "sister in law." She told Eunice that we were getting married. "Your brother just doesn't know it yet." To say that this girl was possessive was putting it mildly. I later found out that this was part of the culture in Puerto Rico. Juanita and I continued to see each other through no choice of mine whatsoever. I was being held hostage in a situation that was totally out of control.

The killing of an innocent and the exodus

I was returning to Harlem one day in the summer of 1964. I was off Broadway and decided to walk ten or twelve blocks before I caught the train uptown. As I approached 64th Street, there was a lot of commotion. An off-duty, plain clothed cop had shot and killed a sixteen year old black child. I found out that some landlord was cleaning the sidewalk and for no reason whatsoever took the hose and sprayed this kid deliberately. The kid shouted at him and maybe cursed him and this racist cop shot and killed him. I became very angry. From all accounts, this was a good kid who never bothered anyone. I was once again witnessing the almost hopeless plight of Blacks in this country. This was a way of life in AmeriKKKa—killing Blacks for no reason. We had no protection from Society, law enforcement, or the United States Government. Later that night, a riot broke out. Huge spotlights were used to blind the crowd. I was definitely not in Charlotte, NC. These New York Blacks were not domesticated and docile like those at home. All hell broke loose. There were garbage cans being thrown from rooftops onto police cars and any other vehicle in sight. They were throwing 78 RPM records with razor blades taped to four sides. Get hit by one of those whirling and you're cut severely. Officers and pedestrians alike were injured. I had never seen anything like this.

It just so happened that momma called me when we finally got home. I told momma what was happening and she put on the performance of her life. She started crying and talking about her baby getting killed. "Please come home, Junior, please come home." I thought about it for a while, I DID NOT want to go back to that g-d d%$#mn Plantation. Edward echoed in. "Man, it's time to get the hell outta Dodge." "I'm not going anywhere, man, you can go." "Man, this is how people get killed, let's go," Edward said. My head was spinning with the sounds of sirens, armored riot cars, blinding lights and violence that I had never witnessed before. I saw people being beaten and policemen bleeding. Finally I relented. "Let's go," I said. We somehow made it to the corner store dodging garbage cans and razors. We got a pound of bologna, a loaf of bread and some mayo. We went back to the house, threw everything in our suitcases. The only way out was to drive directly down 123rd Street through the mayhem to 125th Street on to the Westside Highway. After reaching lower Manhattan it was down to Canal Street through the Holland Tunnel and onto the New Jersey Turnpike. We had survived the riot of 1964. But that experience only added to my anger and resentments towards a system that always allowed brutality towards blacks. After a so-called internal investigation, it was concluded that the officer acted according to regulations and policy. I never remembered a police officer being prosecuted for killing a black person. Like so many others, this officer now had bragging rights. That's the conclusion of ninety-five percent of the reports involving the shooting and killing of Blacks in this society: the officer acted within and according to regulations.

Chapter Fourteen - Back to the G-d Damn Plantation

When I got back to Charlotte, it was even more depressing that when I left. Absolutely nothing had or was going to change. I went back to work at The Charlotte City Club as a waiter. I found an apartment on Dundeen Street. I never believed in roommates so I've always had my own place.

I met Perry, Sonny S, and Henry F at the City Club. We started hanging out, and playing poker at my place. The girls would somehow always be there; my place became the hangout. I was to soon meet William L, a two-bit gangster. He was always moving hot stuff stolen and the traffic always came through my place. When he wasn't moving and storing stolen merchandise, he was jugging. He would sit in a car and wait for someone to come out of a bank with a bank bag. He would then follow the car and wait for the person to either leave the car or would snatch the bag as they were delivering it. One night in 1965, they asked me to drive them to South Carolina. They would pay me $100.00 for my time and gas. That sounded good to me so off we went. We drove to Greenville and I started to become suspicious about this trip. "Park in that lot," one of them said. "We'll be right back." All of a sudden, they came back with arms full of suits. They made four trips. Every inch of space in my car was full of suits. I have never been that afraid in my life. There was no doubt that I wasn't cut out to be a criminal. I was simply too scared. My heart was pounding all the way back. I just knew that there would be a blue light and sirens at any moment. It would be all in the newspaper and six o'clock News. I could clearly see our pictures on the front page.

They were laughing. "You're scared ain't ya?" "Damn right, I'm scared. They'll lock my ass up just because I'm with you guys." I fully understand why so many so-called gangsters are caught. They're as dumb as cornbread, that's why. I mean...I was driving back to Charlotte with a car stuffed with stolen goods. We finally got back to my apartment and unloaded the car. We were knee deep in suits. How they'd gotten 120 of them in my car, I'll never know. The next day William L sold them all to a man who owned a department store in Virginia. William probably got a lot more, but he split $800.00 with us. That pretty much ended my short career in crime. I just wasn't cut out for it. At this point I was using coke, pot and alcohol. We would party hardy two to three times a week. I was losing myself gradually. I continued waiting tables and because the bartender and I were buddies, he would show me how to use the big ginger ale bottles to move liquor. At the large parties and wedding receptions, we would keep the large ginger ale bottles and with a funnel, pour a full fifth of liquor into the bottles while talking to customers or mixing drinks. We were good and would sometimes wind up with a full case of J&B, Johnnie Walker, and Hiram Walker. We didn't fool with the cheap stuff. All we had to do was to account for the empty bottles of liquor and we definitely had the empty bottles.

We would carry the stolen booze to the local nightclubs, charge seventy percent of the face value and keep rolling. We'd always take a fifth home and play poker until the wee hours. This went on until I was about to lose my mind here from the boredom. I missed the excitement of the City.

On November 22, 1965, the homes of Dr. Reginald Hawkins, Kelly Alexander and Attorney Julius Chambers had been bombed. No one had to tell me who did it. These were all civil rights activists. Dr. Hawkins was a stellar example of courage, loyalty, and dedication to the cause of civil rights. Attorney Julius Chambers and Kelly Alexander had been tireless fighters and devout pioneers in the fight for Civil Rights. They were all heroes of mine. I thought about the bombing in Alabama by the same demons who had no regard for life and were so full of hatred.

DC and my first wife

I received a call from Carolyn, an old girlfriend, inviting me to stay in DC with her and her cousin. I left Charlotte again and drove to Washington. I found their place on 44th Street between Benning Road and Dean Avenue. Carolyn worked at the Small Business Administration. Shirley worked at an Army facility at Fort Belvoir as a chemist. She was as smart as they come. Being a waiter, it didn't take me long to find work. I really lucked out. I went to work at the Three Thieves on Wisconsin Avenue in Georgetown. This was by far the most prestigious Restaurant that I'd ever worked at. The power hitters and politicians frequented this place. My favorite customer was soon to become James Hoffa aka Jimmy Hoffa, the president of the Teamsters. This guy was a real bulldog, strictly business. Most of the waiters soon learned not to ask if they could help him. His response was always the same, "Where's Tommy?" "How are you today, Mr. Hoffa?" This was my standard greeting. I had no idea who this gruff, no-nonsense man was until the headwaiter told me. "For God's sake, take good care of this man. Stay away from his table unless he looks up. He does "NOT" want to talk to you or hear any bullshit about how's the family OK? OK. After he's been seated and you've greeted him, tell him, 'When you're ready to order Mr. Hoffa just give me a nod and I'll be there. Will you have a martini today which he always does.' If he answers yes or no, oblige him and he'll look up when he's ready to order. Stay away from his table, don't hang around him or you'll see the other side of him."

I was getting used to seeing influential people like Abraham Ribicoff, Hubert Humphrey, and other prominent politicians. The headwaiter and I hit it off because I knew in order to get the better parties I had to break him off a lil something. He gave me this private party of twenty elderly women who all were dripping in money, furs, and diamonds. All of a sudden this lone man appeared with this unmistakable voice. It was Vincent Price. They all swooned. They thought he was so cool. They drank Dom Perignon and ate bacon-wrapped filet mignons and asparagus. They had escargots as appetizers. I made the Caesar salads in front of them with the romaine lettuce and Parmesan cheese. I mixed the olive oil and vinegar for salad dressing accompanied by crushed anchovies and a raw egg. They had Bananas Foster by candlelight afterwards. To top everything off I served them a demitasse. The bill came to about $745.00. That dinner resulted in the biggest gratuity I had ever received. It was about $185.00, which was a lot of money back then. I shared it with the busboy, the beverage girl and the headwaiter; that's the way business was done.

Somehow, someway, something always drew me back home. After about three months in DC, I headed southbound one more time. I stayed long enough to get Carolyn pregnant; she moved back as well a few months later. We made a decision to get married. I had about as much business getting married as a newborn driving an eighteen-wheeler. I started working at UPS in March of 1967 after they expanded to the south from New York. I was an operations clerk and made the payroll, traced shipments and figured the standards for the drivers. I had no transportation and rode the bus to the terminal daily. I worked about a mile from the bus stop and had to walk the distance. I wanted this job so badly that it didn't matter. I worked second shift but always found someone to give me a ride home around 12:30 AM. Carolyn and I purchased this small home on Kenhill Drive a few months later. The payments were only $79.00 a month and things seemed to be going okay for a while. Her drinking had progressed as well as mine. At first, things were smooth but the mood swings would eventually start. I actually had the nerve to tell her that "she" needed help and this always led to an argument. I couldn't blame her for becoming angry because I was the one who needed help... bad.

Her mother was a dominating person who moved in for three days one Christmas. She was going to surprise us with these great chittlings or so they were supposed to be. This woman had a bright idea of putting about thirty pounds of salt along with half a can of sage in the chittlings. She f-ck-d those chittlings up royally. I was really looking forward to those bad boys. I had prepared the coleslaw and rice impeccably. I also hooked up some killer cornbread. I was mad as hell with that woman. You couldn't eat the damn things regardless of how drunk you were. The two of them threatened to jump on me and they would have so I left for a while, a long while. I always ran when challenges or problems arose. My inability to handle personal responsibility created most of my problems. I had two children and one on the way. I was not even twenty-three years old. The future became dimmer and more frightening. After five years of experimental marriage, I couldn't go any farther. I did what I did best. I ran. I left for good. I gave her everything: the house, the furniture...everything.

Chapter Sixteen -UPS and the Climb Upward

I was still working at United Parcel Service and doing a very good job. I went through a lot of mixed emotions. I felt guilty because Steven was only five years old and I was taking the easy way out. I continued to see Steven and I knew that Carolyn was hoping for reconciliation. The only thing worse than a person with a substance problem is two people with substance problems. I had been moving so fast those past twenty-seven years that everything seemed to be a blur. I did everything to escape the past. I couldn't stop thinking of my two little girls—wherever they were, Mary, Carla, Gin, my father; to escape my family, and finally...myself. While I stuck to my routine at work, I was staying to myself more and more. I was alone with my jazz, black lights, and florescent fishnets in the ceiling. While my place was cool and a safe refuge, I was becoming very uncool. I was establishing a reputation as a playboy, but nothing was farther from the truth. What I realize today is that the basic need of any human being, whether infant, toddler or adult, is simply to be loved and to love in return. I was starting to question my ability to love and being capable of accepting love. I carried myself like the most confident person in the world. People still tell me this today. I've always had a lot of confidence because of my faith in God. I believe that faith produces courage and that courage produces confidence.

The guilt started to overwhelm me and my thoughts more and more were those of a coward and failure. I started to feel that maybe I was incapable of loving or being loved. I could escape the thoughts of being alone on the days that I went to work. I enjoyed being at work; I enjoyed my job. The Northerners that I worked with were just different; there was always humor. I had been doing such a good job with the payroll, the standards, and tracing shipments that after only two years, management approached me. They wanted me to become a driver trainer. Little did I know that I was being prepped for supervision. I couldn't even drive a truck, but I learned extremely fast and actually started a route within a few months. I was master of the numbers and was creative. I created the numbers necessary for me to be a super star everyday. It wasn't long at all before I was training the new drivers and in the fast track for supervision. I could actually go home daily and take a nap if I chose to while the other drivers caught hell simply going to the bathroom.

I worked hard, but I also worked smart. I would make a stop at Union Carbide on Reames Road and say it was a multiple—making several deliveries in the same building. I would buy the receiving clerk lunch once a week and he would sign for everything, giving me extra credits. I found out early in life that when people like you things go so much smoother in every area of life because they'll do things for you that they wouldn't do for difficult people. I kept my appearance impeccable, and my truck as well. The trucks would be washed daily because UPS believed in having the cleanest equipment on the road. I swept my vehicle out daily and kept the windshield cleaned from the inside. This meant the world to people who were looking at you, especially the customers. I was out delivering in Mallard Creek this particular day going towards David Cox Road. I was going into a curve when all of a sudden, as I was turning into the curve, the steering wheel was going in circles. Something in the steering mechanism had broken and I was heading straight towards this big ditch. When I hit the ditch the truck fell on it's side and was sliding through a fence. The cows ran for their lives. I held on for dear life as the truck slid for over 100 feet. I was shaken but otherwise unhurt.

A neighbor called emergency medics and UPS. It was in a flash that an ambulance and fire truck were on the scene. UPS must have jetted out there because they were there almost as fast as the emergency vehicles. The emblems on the truck were covered because we wanted to maintain our safe driving image. By company policy, I was automatically suspended for three days pending an investigation. It didn't take them long to realize that it was mechanical failure and not driver negligence that caused the accident. I think what impressed the Company most was the fact that I didn't attempt to claim injuries and enlist an attorney. This was the assurance they needed that I was a "good" Company man. I was now on the fast track with UPS. I continued delivering and was now the super driver.

Emma my wife and savior

Cold Budweiser and pork rinds were calling my name. I couldn't wait to get back to the comfort and coolness of my apartment, Carlos Santana and Elton John. After completing paperwork and checking out, I was leaving the terminal and the first person I saw was Peggy. She was waiting for Ronnie, her boyfriend, in the parking lot. As I waved I noticed another girl with her and casually spoke. We chatted for a while and flirted with each other big time. We were soon dating. Emma and I had great times going to dinner, movies, and parties. We almost became inseparable. She was either at my place or I at hers. We lived off of West Boulevard about a mile or so apart. People started asking me, "How's Emma," when they saw me because they were accustomed to seeing us together. I wanted more than anything for this to work and to stick forever. I was so tired of running especially from things that were good for me. We spent quality time together and she was an incredible cook. Those were during the days that we ate pig feet, cornbread, and rice—real soul food. We kicked it real well together and I couldn't wait to get home every day so that I could call her and just talk.

One day she asked me, "Why don't you come home with me this weekend and meet my folk?" This sounded great to me so off we went. We went to a little town out of Lancaster, SC called Heath Springs. As we passed by the jail that was hardly bigger than a closet we laughed about this sho nuff being the country, but I loved it. Her family and I got along very well. I liked her mother, her sister, and four brothers. I really enjoyed going down to the country; it was so relaxing and quiet. Charlotte was fast, furious and violent. Her uncle used to go to the white theaters during segregation because he was so light. We laughed about this all the time. These people were the same everyday; they never changed and didn't know anything about being phony. In the spring and early summer the honeysuckles were so fragrant and relaxing. I could nap at her momma's house like nowherc else. That country breeze coming through her window was wonderful and I caught up on much needed rest and sleep. After a while I would hear the sizzling chicken being prepared and the aroma was enough to wake the dead.

One thing led to another and after a year I realized how much I loved Emma. I wanted her to be my wife. I bought an engagement ring and made it official. My groomsmen were mostly from UPS. Emma invited classmates, friends, and a few relatives to be bridesmaids. I'll never forget the rehearsal at this little country church down the street from her mother's house. We had a ball. All the guys stayed overnight at the motel. The only thing that I remember about that night was that we laughed, smoked joints, and drank. The wedding took place. Everyone was happy and smiling as big as Texas. The flowers, the preacher, and everyone there created a holy atmosphere. Emma glowed and was drop dead beautiful. Ours was a healthy relationship, we were a happy family, and I had a very promising career with UPS. All was right with the world. We stayed in Little Rock Apartments for a while, but the Company wanted me to move from there. This was not a place they wanted a future manager to live in. They were right; I needed to be in a better neighborhood. We started looking for our first home and found it in Hidden Valley. This was the largest Black sub division in Charlotte. Emma was pregnant with our first child, Thomas, and I was excited about being a real father this time. When she delivered him, I recorded him before he was even washed up. I was so proud of our little boy. Thomas had a little nursery in the bedroom of our apartment and we were like three peas in a pod.

Emma and I were at home talking one night when all of a sudden we heard a crash in Thomas' bedroom. It was the sound of breaking glass. We rushed to our baby to find some bastard had thrown a brick through his window. I saw a person running through the woods behind our house. I rushed to get my rifle, ran outside, and fired off six rounds trying my best to hit the bastard at least once. As Emma called the police, I knew it was futile; they'd be useless. All the same, I told them about this two-bit punk who wanted to be a gangster. I either had witnessed something or knew of a crime that he was involved in and this was just a form of intimidation; or so he thought. I shared all of this information with the police but nothing ever came of it. They never caught the person who threw the brick. We stayed on Mt Kisco Drive for maybe three months when the Company wanted me to transfer to Greenville, SC. No problem, I knew what to expect when I went into supervision. I was totally about company and becoming an executive manager with them one day. Emma was with me all the way. We joked that the unpacked boxes were ready for the next move.

I remained a driver-supervisor for about 3-4 months and then went into the personnel department. I started traveling over North and South Carolina. I was doing much of the hiring. I conducted eight-hour orientations for the new people back in Charlotte about once a month. I would stay on the road sometimes for months but was generally home on the weekends. Now I wore a shirt and tie every day and felt more like a professional. Soon, I was carrying the American Express Platinum card, Diners Club and was loaded with good credit.

In the motel rooms I'd read up on policy and procedures to stay abreast of everything going on and to have answers when asked at anytime about UPS. I had many temptations on the road but I had no problem staying as far away from them as possible. It was business at all times. Some of the women I encountered were gorgeous but I was a married man and I knew there were many eyes on me. I'm sure that most guys in personnel face these temptations all the time. I'm also sure that many have lost their careers because of stupidity. I was happy with my marriage, the company, and life in general. I was not going to risk my job over anything.

This particular night in Greensboro NC after a long day at work, I had a drink, smoked a joint, and relaxed watching the news. I was a scotch drinker now and smoked casually. After about an hour or so I thought to myself to call home and see if everything was okay. I was reaching for the phone when all of a sudden there was a very sharp, what seemed to be an electric shock in my left arm. It shot down my entire arm. Then, a terrible pain hit my lower back. It hit me so hard that I fell back on the bed and was literally paralyzed for at least three minutes. My breathing was short and labored. I couldn't reach the telephone to call for help and couldn't talk. I stayed on that bed totally helpless for what seemed an eternity. After a while the pain subsided and I was somewhat normal again. I didn't even have sense enough to call the operator or go to the hospital. A person with a third grade education would have immediately gone to the hospital or at least called someone to take them there. I was much too macho; I figured I would tell my doctor about it when I got back to Charlotte. I did, but it took me twenty years.

It's amazing how drug users trivialize life-threatening situations. I prescribed my own remedy. I immediately gave up the cigarettes. I lost weight as well. I weighed about 202 pounds. The only problem was that a lot of this weight was concentrated around my waist. I started eating salads and plenty of them. I'm not sure that I even told Emma what happened. I easily could have died in that motel room. When I look back it was probably my blood pressure, which has always been high and unstable. I went home for the weekend, and spent quality time with Emma and Thomas.

I had many good drivers but there was one very bad seed whom I was convinced was a hardcore racist and a psychopath. They called him the Hawk. At times he could be tolerable, other times he was sarcastic and evil. He had the same look as Charles Manson. He definitely didn't like blacks or anyone else who wasn't white. One night I was outside the terminal and he was coming in from his route mad as hell. He thought his load was too heavy and was ranting and raving. He actually tried to run over me. He called me a nigger but made sure there were no witnesses. I reported this to the terminal manager who was very indifferent.

"Don't pay Hawk no attention, he's like that," he said.

"Self preservation is the first law of nature," I reminded him. "If he continue this nonsense, there's going to be trouble."

Well, the problems continued. He would yell out on the loading belt in the morning that he was bringing back stops because he wasn't going that way today. Sure enough he bought back deliveries he didn't make. This had to stop like fast, quick and in a hurry. The consequences of this could start an all out revolt and a bad pattern with the other drivers.

When this news got back to the District office, guess who they held responsible? Yep, you guessed it. They claimed that I was the professional and should have handled it differently.

"How would you have handled it?" I asked them. "Maybe you would have jumped in between a different truck to avoid being run over?"

They knew the score but this was how racism operated—on a subtle level. If the situation had been reversed and that had been a white supervisor and a black driver, the black driver would have been fired on the spot. This was the best Company that I had ever worked for but in the end, I was black and the driver was white. The workers also had an incredible union, the Teamsters. Life is funny sometimes. I was thinking for a fleeting moment how I served the top dog of the Teamsters back in Washington DC, Jimmy Hoffa, and now I found myself at odds not with his organization but my own company.

I had gotten into Amway and found energy I never knew I had. I had these visions of making big money and becoming independent. I would leave the terminal after a thirteen-hour day and drive forty miles sometimes to Clemson, SC to meet and draw circles explaining how Amway worked. Sometimes I wouldn't get home until 11:00 PM. I talked to God the entire drive there and back. Emma knew that I was being faithful and loyal to her and would always welcome me home with a hug and a kiss. I got by on five hours of sleep and would wake up in the morning refreshed.

At this point I got transferred again—to Anderson, SC, thirty miles south of Greenville. This was punishment because I actually drove right by the Greenville terminal going to Anderson. I now had to leave home at 5:45 AM to get to the terminal by 6:45 AM. It didn't matter because I was so pumped up on "Think and Grow Rich" by Napoleon Hill, "The Magic of Thinking Big" and "The Power of Positive Thinking" that I would dream of success and envision that motor home I'd drive across the country all the way to work. As it turns out, the move was good for me. The terminal manager was a better person, but I had to start all over again with new drivers.

It didn't take me long to figure out that transfers was the way the Companies dealt with people that they want to become totally submissive. I didn't know what I had done to deserve this but I kept doing the best job that I knew how to do. If a driver were out for any reason, I would gladly deliver his route. I loved being on my own and traveling through Abbeville, Greenwood, Ninety Six, and Belton SC.

I delivered a package to this very old doctor's office and was told to bring it to the back door. I actually saw signs that read white's waiting room and Negro waiting room. I couldn't believe it. This was in 1975 and these people were still living Jim Crow.

Emma and I found this great house in a neighborhood that the Realtor tried to steer us away from. It was a White neighborhood. I didn't care what color the neighborhood was. I knew that I earned the money, was qualified to make the monthly mortgage payment and everything else was moot. I knew exactly what the neighbors expected from us but boy did we knock their socks off. The first project was to create a new yard with heavy seeding. We then purchased palm trees, exotic flowers and kept the shrubs manicured. Our yard was not only the most beautiful in the neighborhood but would easily rank in the top fifty in the city. At first they would throw beer cans and bottles in the yard but when we created that showcase yard, people started stopping and asking how in the world we kept that yard so beautiful. People actually started waving, and the harassment pretty much stopped.

On the weekends we would go to the farmers market and browse for hours. I carried little Thomas in a papoose on my back everywhere we went. For once in my life I was in a healthy relationship, had a son and we were a real family. It felt so good to be faithful, loyal, and yoked together with a woman that I loved. I was proud of myself, and my little family. When I look back, this was the only time since taking that first drink at momma's that I could enjoy a sociable drink and stop.

One day I was training a driver on The Greenwood-Abbeville route, I noticed these people riding in these little horse drawn buggies. After inquiring, I was told that they were Mennonites. Riding past their communities, I noticed how they appeared to have been locked in the past. There were no cars and they worked the gardens manually. They were extremely close knit and stayed to themselves.

The Mennonites had a restaurant in Abbeville and served the freshest foods and vegetables from their own gardens. The food was absolutely the best on the planet. The macaroni and cheese was heavenly and the vegetables were out of this world. They were cooked and seasoned to perfection. They were such humble and respectful people. They were about helping people at all times. I wondered why the whole world couldn't adopt their standards of living and coexistence. There was no racism in their community, period. Of course, there were no Blacks either.

I was attracted to these people because of their kindness and attitude towards others. The only other group that I respect and admire is the Quakers. I know how hard they fought for and with Blacks in that evil and heinous system known as chattel slavery. I began to notice that the terminal manager would criticize me for small things. It was almost like a bully starting a fight. We started having heated discussions about the most trivial things. I sensed that my time was up and that I had become a marked man. It was really about Amway. Word was out that I was doing well and my sponsorships were growing. I guess looking back in retrospect it was a conflict of interest. I only wished that they had simply told me my business was a conflict and given me a choice. I was on a hit list now.

Things were tense and stress had started taking its toll at work. Then the bombshell dropped. In January 1977 I was told to report to the district office back in Charlotte. I was smart enough to know that I wasn't receiving a medal or commendation for outstanding service. I met with the District Manager who said, "Your services are no longer required." I had a gut feeling of what to expect. I was smart enough to draft a letter that I would take to an attorney, send to the corporate office, the EEOC (which is a joke), The Charlotte Observer, and the office of the North Carolina Attorney General.

I gave the letter to the manager and went back to Anderson. The letter detailed the discrimination that I had experienced not only in driving from Greenville to Anderson everyday, but the past four years. I received a phone call from the District Office almost as soon as I walked through the terminal door back in Anderson. He wanted me to come back to Charlotte in a couple of days to see if we could straighten this out. That letter had changed everything.

When I went back to Charlotte, I was assured that everything had been straightened out and that I was still an employee. I thought about it there in the office and realized that I would never be happy anywhere because I wanted to call the shots and be an entrepreneur. I actually resigned, which was premature. Being an addict, I always created mountains out of molehills out of someone spilling a little salt from the shaker. There's no way that I should have left that wonderful company. The matter would have blown over in a few weeks. I'm not like a lot of folks who demean and downgrade companies for terminating them. I call it like it is, and what happened to me was just business. It's true that Blacks historically have been brutalized, traumatized, and discriminated against but there are some companies, like people, who try to do what's right. Being fair about the situation, I can honestly say that UPS was and still is a good company. In fact, I can honestly say that it's the best company I've ever worked for.

The problem was me, and my distorted perception of things. No one was after me; they just wanted my complete loyalty to the company. Thinking about it now, I'd want the same thing from my employees if I were calling the shots. I was much too hasty walking away from that job. I went home and told my wife what I had done. She was still in my corner; she always supported me in whatever I decided to do. I rented a U Haul, loaded that baby, and drove it back to Charlotte to our new home on Vickery Drive in Hampshire Hills. My drinking had once again become frequent. The dream of owning and operating a restaurant was conceived. I had been a good waiter and bartender. Why not?

Emma kept an immaculate house and Thomas was about four years old. We decided that he needed a playmate, a little sister or brother. Little Levon was on the planning board. We looked around and finally found this abandoned building on West Blvd near Remount Road. We inquired about the building and finally met and talked to this Greek man about a property that his company owned on the west side of town. We signed the lease. I was dumb as cornbread when it came to business but we were excited about the possibility of becoming restaurant moguls. I had to meet with building inspectors, the health department, electricians, and plumbers. I had no idea how strict codes were. Incidentally, Emma was quite pregnant with little Lee and she worked so hard. We were painting, washing windows, scrubbing floors and just about everything that had to be done.

In the course of going to the hardware store to purchase nails, paint and other items needed for repair, this particular day I was riding up West Boulevard and noticed this guy painting and working on his business. I would stop and chat with him and we both talked about opening our little restaurants. He told me his name was Richard and I admired him working everyday painting, cleaning windows, planning to for his grand opening. He told me that his business was going to be fast food, I shared with him that mine would be full service with dinners and a bar. Today his business is called Bojangles, and mine is long gone. I don't dwell on this but that the toll drug usage extracts is horrendous. It takes everything, leaving total and complete failure, as you will soon see.

Chapter Seventeen - Dancing with the Demon

In July, 1975, five months after leaving UPS, Emma and I opened a restaurant that we called Tommy's. This was absolutely the greatest plan for failure known to mankind. Because of my inability to plan and project anything related to business, I devised a plan for total failure. It was definitely a mom and pop venture that we started with less than a fifth of what should have been required capitol. We never had enough money, or a back-up plan; we were trusting my good intentions. They tell me that the road to failure is paved with good intentions. I proved it.

After a month or so of preps, being approved by the Government agencies and acquiring seating and all pots, pans and utensils, we opened. The grand opening was a natural, or should I say a man-made disaster. This woman that I had hired, who had worked at other food establishments before, sent out lettuce that was brown and old, chicken and rolls that were burnt and the customers definitely showed it to me. I had invited city hall in for my grand opening and I felt horrible.

Remember, because of my inability to accept personal responsibility, I pretty much created every problem that I had. I realized that I was the one who should have been in the kitchen all along, or at least had a seasoned professional. I had the expertise to cook very well and could handle dealing with eight sandwiches at once. This was a case of one person trying to wear four different hats and not being efficient at any. I either needed a seasoned manager or a good cook. I couldn't do both, but I tried.

This man stopped by one day after lunch was over. I realized that he was John Mc Donald, a man known all over Charlotte as the owner and operator of McDonald Cafeteria, the most famous Black restaurant in Charlotte. He was a good Christian man who believed in virtuous living and God's word. He was trying to give me some of the best advice I've ever received, even until today.

He knew that I had applied for liquor by the drink. This would license and permit me to store and sell liquor by the drink to the public.

He told me flat out, "Son, this will be the worst mistake that you'll make while on this corner."

How prophetic those words would turn out to be. Jimmy Mc Key and I would be the only blacks in the entire city that were awarded the permits at that time. Jimmy Mc Key was the owner and proprietor of the famed Excelsior Club. I'd go to the Alcoholic Beverage Control warehouse or the ABC store to purchase liquor just like groceries. We had items on the menu that people couldn't even pronounce. This was my first mistake, having food, like Beef Stroganoff, that the people couldn't identify with. Other mistakes would follow. The average Joe, or even not so average, wouldn't order what they couldn't pronounce.

The next mistake was under-pricing the food. People with no knowledge of business either charge too much or too little. My third mistake was that the part of town in which we were located was not a sociable liquor-by-the drink community. This was West Boulevard where people didn't raise glasses; they raised hell.

The fourth, and worse mistake, was the fact that the owner and proprietor himself was an addict. One of the neighbors, who also owned a store across the street, was the neighborhood drug dealer. Naturally, he visited sometimes to establish a new client. The new client would soon become his best client. More and more of the restaurant's profits went up my nose. It was the 70s and I was exploring new adventures in the drug arena.

The business started selling more and more liquor and less food. It was becoming known as a bar. I was selling just enough food to satisfy the ABC board's requirements. Emma would sometimes leave early so as not to be on her feet too long, being as pregnant as she was. Women were hitting on me from all angles in the later hours, especially after two or three drinks.

This Irish woman who was in marketing with this radio station was stopping by local businesses passing out contest forms that they were sponsoring. I remember her ordering a Tom Collins, and then another. After the second one, she started getting real friendly. Lionel Ritchie was on the radio singing, "Three Times a Lady." She asked me to take her on a tour of the kitchen.

There was nothing to tour. It was a simple kitchen, a walk-in fridge, and a storage room. It was becoming very evident what she really wanted. As she started unbuttoning her blouse, someone came in.

"Is it too late to order a sandwich?"

"Never!" I said. It could just as well been anyone, including my wife. I simply had an absence of morals and principles at that time. Drugs ruled and had started controlling every aspect of my life. Eventually, Emma did come. Through her eyes, this woman was the same as a Jezebel in Church. From that day forward Emma had suspicions that were totally justified. I had become a womanizer. I was in the restaurant from 9AM until 11PM. The Bible says that the spirit is strong but the flesh is weak. So true. I've always wanted to do the right thing but I was slowly losing my dignity—my oneness with God.

In the interim, Emma and I fixed that old house up very well. We wallpapered, painted, and cleaned the windows immaculately. Emma was a very neat woman who worked very hard in that house to keep it spotless. All of this was done in preparation for our little girl soon to be born. We had her little room all prepared. It was a beautiful 950 square foot little home.

The business had somewhat stabilized. We were paying the bills and the creditors were satisfied The Irish woman had left a book of coupons for this trip to New Orleans. My niece took the whole book home and put her name on them all. She used her name but she was much too young to go to New Orleans. When the woman came back, she announced that LaTonda had won but that she would have to transfer the trip to someone who was of legal age. She gave the trip to Emma and me.

We were ecstatic and planned our four day getaway to The Big Easy. We flew Delta's new L10-11, which was their biggest wide body jet. We arrived in New Orleans after leaving little Thomas with his grandmother in Heath Springs. We were greeted at the Royal Sonesta where we had a suite. I only wished that Emma had not been so uncomfortable because she was still very pregnant. Her doctor had told her not to travel but there was no way I was going to New Orleans alone.

New Orleans became the first on my list of places "not" to visit. It was just a bunch of drunks, weirdoes, and very loose people parading the streets. In addition it was hot and humid as hell. The food was superb and the jazz music was exceptional. There was really nothing to do except drink, walk and sweat. After returning to Charlotte, Emma gave birth to my little girl Levon (pronounced Lee-vone).

I was a big Elton John fan and still am to this day. I had his album "Madman Across the Water." On it, he sang about Levon. It really didn't matter what or who the song was about, I fell in love with the song and the sound of Levon. I later found out that Levon was a boy. We played with that little girl. Emma and I sometimes playfully argued about someone holding her too long because it was "my" turn. It's amazing that we didn't pull her apart because whoever had her wouldn't let go. If I wanted her to squeal and laugh, I would blow on that little belly. She was the softest, sweetest smelling little thing in the world. I loved to put her little cheek next to mine and just love her to death, just like my daddy did with us. Thomas loved her to death. He stayed glued to his little sister. That same love exists between these two today, as when Lee was born.

Levon was just months old when that day in infamy would arrive. I was in the restaurant talking to the staff when this guy rushes in breathless.

He desperately asked, "Who's TOMMY? Who's TOMMY?"

"I am," I said.

"I've got some bad news, man, I hate to tell you this but…" He was trying to catch his breath, taking what seemed to be forever to tell me what it was.

"What's wrong, man, what's wrong?" I demanded. Tell me what is it!"

"Your son has been hit by a car!"

I ran home as fast as I could with him on my heels. When I turned the corner I saw every emergency vehicle known to man. There were police cars, an ambulance, and fire trucks all with flashing lights. The closer I got I recognized Emma holding what seemed to be a bloody rag doll in her arms. She was delirious. The little rag doll was my little boy, Thomas. I knew that I had to be stronger than I'd ever been before. I called on God as I ran towards them. I asked Him to save my little boy. I couldn't even recognize my precious, beautiful little boy. His face was literally torn from his jawbone and scalp. You could see the actual blood vessels in his face and scalp.

Both of his legs were broken at the top and bottom, he had contusions, concussions, and fractured everything. I didn't know what to say or do but I saw more compassion from a mother in those few minutes than I had in my entire life. I tried my absolute best to console my wife and child. His eyes were searching and darting about frantically. The look of horror and fear on my child's face was indescribable.

He was only five years old. I'll never know how he withstood the pain and trauma to this day. It was only the grace and mercy of a living God that my son survived. Had he landed on the asphalt, I don't think he would have lived through it. It was God's grace that he landed on grass.

The emergency technicians were quick to tell us, "Your son has less than a forty percent chance of arriving at the hospital alive. He's totally paralyzed and in severe shock."

Thomas had darted out from a parked car and couldn't see the oncoming traffic. The car hit him, as tiny as he was, broadside from his neck down. The car tossed him forty feet down the street into a neighbors yard. When we arrived at the hospital the triage team was waiting and frantically started to work on him.

One after another, all the nurses asked, "Is there was anything I can do?"

I spoke words that were not my own. "Where's the chapel?" I went into that chapel and asked God to SPEAK to me personally. I prayed what most people would have prayed. "Please don't take my little boy. I will go wherever you want me to go; do whatever you want me to do." I realize today that God can't be bargained with.

Still I prayed. "Forgive me my sins, God. Shelter our little boy from further harm and damage. God, please guide the surgeons' hands, their thoughts, and decisions."

I realized that I was giving God dictation and stopped. Finally, I said, "Thy will be done, Lord God." All the same, I asked Him to place one of his angels in the midst of the operating team and that regardless of my request that His will be done.

At that point, I felt like the most unworthy man in the world. I was a drug user, but I knew that God knew I was a good person who needed help the same as my father had needed help. When I came out of that chapel for what seemed to be an eternity, I knew beyond the shadow of a doubt that Thomas would be fine. I remembered the preachers saying that when you know that you know that you know, all is well. And I knew that my son would be okay.

The doctor came to Emma and me. "There's better than a sixty percent chance that your little boy will not survive surgery. He's in extremely critical condition and his vitals are slipping."

I told him emphatically, "Our son will be fine. He's going to be fine."

They looked at me as though I was crazy. The stare I received from them almost froze time. It was a look of disbelief. I did not waver.

The surgeon decided to give me his version of hope. "If he survives, he will probably be a paraplegic or suffer some major form of paralysis."

I turned a deaf ear to all of them. I believed that God was telling me "Don't listen to them my son, I am with you." Thomas not only survived the many hours of surgery, he survived through intensive care for eight days. He was fitted with a crown, a device that kept his head in a permanent position for weeks until they could determine whether paralysis was in any part of his body.

His mother kept a vigil. She loved her children so much and would gladly have killed a bear to protect them. I was there to the best of my ability. I still had a restaurant to run. Thomas started moving arms, legs, then toes and everything. I remember going into the bathroom weeping because of this loving, caring and compassionate God who sits high and looks low. He gave us back our son. He's always been there for me. I felt so guilty about my drug use and saw myself as a total failure. God saved my life in that motel room and in that horrible accident years before. Now again, God answered my prayer. What many people would consider a curse, God's grace turned tragedy into a blessing. Quite simply, my son could have been dead on arrival or at best, a paraplegic for life.

"Thank you Lord, thank you for touching my son on that day." Our little boy is now thirty-three years old and strong as an ox. He can also eat like an ox and never gains an ounce. He has hardly any visible scars on his face or scalp. After about eight weeks of care, Thomas was ready to go home with us, body cast and all. I had to carry him around with my hand on his back and the other on his body cast. That's when my mother's humor kicked in and I remembered the quote from Shakespeare that "laughter is the best tonic." I devised a strategy that let him watch as much comedy and cartoons that he could stand. When I had the chance, I watched with him. Man, we laughed and laughed. He was always itching so we had to figure a way to scratch those little legs down in the body cast. I rigged a clothes hanger wrapped in cloth and slid it back and forth in the cast.

We would take him outside and lay him on a blanket so his playmates could come over and talk to him and play little games with him. Can you imagine the feeling that a parent has when they see for the first time their child laughing after such an excruciating ordeal? Children are the most amazing creatures in the world; their innocence is unparalleled. Their resilience is remarkable. We talked to his doctor who told us that the family needed to take a fun vacation together somewhere like the beach after the body cast is removed.

Finally the cast was taken off. He went to therapy to relearn how to walk. About four weeks later, we planned a vacation. I wanted to take the family somewhere different, somewhere other than Myrtle Beach. I had heard a lot about Hilton Head Island. My son, Steven, was about ten years old and living with his mother. We took him with us.

I mapped the trip. We would go down I-77 to Columbia and then take I-26 to I-95 South. We would take the Hilton Head exit for about 56 miles, cross the bridge and be there. It was truly a sight to see, we had this big carrier on top of the car, two kids in the back, Emma, myself, and little Levon in the front. We were rolling down the highway Beverly Hillbillies style. We arrived in Hilton Head to a torrential downpour. It floods quickly in the low country and we were actually driving through what seemed to be a lake.

We finally got established. Everyone wanted to hold Levon, especially Steven. He loved his little sister to death. I had already charted my strategy for Thomas about how I would take the crutches away from him. He struggled with those crutches anyhow; they were so awkward because they were too big for him. The next day on the beach his mother raised a big fuss with me about forcing her little boy to walk without his crutches and how it was paining him to do so. He did cry for a while but with outstretched arms and a lot of coaxing, I persuaded him to "come on Thomas, come on."

The wobbly tiny steps grew an inch each time. He was gaining confidence in his ability to walk. I knew that it hurt him but I also knew that this would be one of the greatest gifts that we could give him—the ability to walk on his own, no canes, no crutches or any other walking aids despite the doctor's prophesy of a wheelchair for life. God didn't agree with them; neither did I. Remember Napoleon Hill? "What the mind of man can conceive and believe, it can achieve." God was giving us back our little boy.

We had a good time at the beach. We caught shrimp, fish and crabs in the inlet, then, I'd prepare my version of a seafood platter for the family. We went to Harbor Town and saw what it was like to be amongst the rich and famous. I was trying to instill the ability in my children to become dreamers. I wanted them to conceive, believe, and achieve whatever they chose to become. We saw the biggest yachts, the most expensive homes and for my first time, a Lamborghini. I had never in my life seen that kind of living. The rich have this way of looking right through you, as though you don't exist. There's never an acknowledgement of your presence—unless you're one of them.

When we left that Island, I became an even bigger dreamer. We got back to Charlotte, reopened the restaurant, and the beat went on. Coke became more and more prevalent. Thank God that my wife never partook. She was an excellent example of a woman and a mother but my values were becoming more and more distorted. I don't remember using or taking any drugs on our trip. It felt good to function as a father. This wouldn't last long; the demon was calling long before we reached Charlotte. I was changing. My new god would be cocaine. In the summer of 1979 we went to New York City to visit Emma's sister and brother-in-law in Laurelton Queens. Bob took us on a tour of New York City and all the memories came back. Everything was still there. We drove up to Milford Connecticut to play Jai Lai. I couldn't lose and won a $1,000.00. We went back to Queens loaded. Take one guess as to what I insisted on doing the next day? You're right; I wanted to go back. Despite everyone telling me not to do it, they relented. I drove back up. Take another guess as to what happened? You're right again. I gave every nickel back. It was a very quiet ride back this time.

The next day I received a phone call. There had been a fire at the restaurant. The fire investigator quizzed me thoroughly. It appeared that arson was the cause. "Can you think of enemies, motives, and any other reason someone would do this?" I could think of nothing. They still suspected me of being involved though. I was issued a paltry check for $10,000 that went entirely to the Small Business Administration. This was the end of the restaurant and I was officially unemployed. We were penniless. There was no money for another start up. I blame myself for not seeking a more dedicated attorney but attorneys who cared about the business of blacks were few. Blacks and the poor are cheated out of so much simply because they don't know their rights or seek expert advice. My son's settlement ($10,000) with Allstate was negotiated through two of these attorneys. One was the same one who negotiated the insurance settlement for the restaurant. Supposedly acting on our behalf, he was simply acting in concert with Allstate's attorney. This settlement represented the full amount that Thomas would receive for the rest of his natural life.

Today I become very angry about how much money those bastards put in their pockets in return for depriving my son the care that he would require in future years. Today my son's back literally kills him and he can't perform manual work because of the debilitating back pain. There is no help for him at all and he can't get insurance. I should have remembered what people always told me. "Never trust a white man." How right they were. They twisted our arms and hounded Emma and me to settle for this goddamn pocket change at our little boy's expense. I'll always wonder how much Allstate gave them under the table. I'll never understand once again how they slept at night. Today I know that racists don't have consciences. Thomas was left high and dry. When he became eighteen, the money was his. He could do with it whatever he chose to do. He chose to spend every dime of it with his buddies at the beach and wherever else. There I was: broke, unemployed, and as Bobby Blue Bland said, "Three Steps from the Blues."

Chapter Nineteen - Meeting the Demon Face to Face

One day after being out of work a few months, I saw an old acquaintance from Fairview Homes named Magdalene, the devil's daughter. Her name may as well have been Beelzebub. She invited me to her house that evening. Everyone was sitting at her kitchen table smoking something I didn't have a clue about. Little did I know that in front of me was the Demon in the form of a little white rock. Mag yelled at this brother at the table. "Git yo broke ass up nigger and git the hell outta heah; let Tommy sit down. You takin up space wid yo beggin ass." He pleaded to her, "Mag gimme one mo baby, I'll pay you Friday you know I will." Mag gave him a deadly look and screamed at him. "If I haff to tell you one mo goddamn time, I'm gon git my pistol and bust a cap in yo ass. Now git to gittin!" The brother was near tears as he dragged himself out the door, which slammed behind him. Another guy hit the pipe and grinded his teeth something awful. I looked at Mag and whispered to her, "Why the hell is he grinding his teeth like that?" Suddenly, she yelled out "STOP GRINDING YO GODDAMN TEETH FOOL, YOU RUNNIN US CRAZY AS HELL, STOP IT." She was actually grinding her teeth too.

Mag's mood changed in a twinkling of an eye as she smiled broadly at me with the few teeth she had left. She had a small pipe and lit it for me. There was a small rock like substance in the bowl of the pipe. The taste was slightly sweet and the smoke that it produced was white as snow. She told me to hit it softly and slowly. When I did, something happened that exceeded any orgasm that I had ever experienced twenty fold. It was such an incredible rush and a sense of total euphoria. Every cell, tissue, and drop of blood in my body was alive, energized; I felt perfect in everyway. I developed an erection that felt as though it would rip my pants open. I was in love with the entire world and could have kissed my worst enemy, even a Klansman. I knew beyond the shadow of a doubt that at that moment, I was in more trouble than I'd ever been in my life. I was dancing with the demon and he had a grip on me that would take twelve years to break. I was literally paralyzed in that chair for hours and couldn't leave that house until three o'clock in the morning. I wasn't paralyzed in the sense that I couldn't move, but I was transfixed to the pipe and refused to leave. I wanted more and refused to leave until they put me out. My money was all gone and I was hooked on something that would make heroin, cocaine, alcohol, and all the rest seem like aspirin. I was without question instantly hooked.

I got home and couldn't explain where I'd been. Emma was left to her own devices to figure out if I'd been with a woman or whatever. My biggest regret today is that I put her through so much misery and pain. I would pray, "Lord God, please help me to stop this, please sir, help me." My wife was the only one working and I was totally useless and becoming more hopeless as the days went by.

I became a fixture at Magdalene's, even though I really didn't want to be there. At that point, I had no choice. What seemed to be a cute little monkey clanging the cute little symbols and dancing for coins had become a six hundred pound gorilla with a terrible attitude and a very mean spirit. The only difference is that the gorilla was giving orders now. He told me specifically that changes had been made in company policy.

The first change was that from now on was I would be doing the damn dancing and would only take orders from him. "Don't make any plans before consulting with me first," he told me.

The second change, he said, is, "I will be the most important thing in your life—before God, children, and your wife as well."

I knew I would obey. I slid deeper and deeper into a black hole of despair. I was seeing first hand how my father must have felt not being able to talk to anyone about this horror. My mother and father had divorced in the mid eighties and he moved to a seniors' house on East Morehead Street. I would visit my dad and saw vividly how the accident had made him a totally different man. He never touched alcohol or cigars again. If momma had just held on a little while longer, she would have had the man she knew he could be. He absolutely adored all of his grandchildren. He loved Tiffany, LaTonda, Antoine, Thomas, and Levon. As long as he could hold their hands with both his hands, he was happy. He loved to bounce them on his good knee. I often wondered what it meant to old folk to hold someone' hand with both of theirs.

Momma married this man whom none of us liked. His name was Alexander and for the most part, he was worse than my father had ever been. He wasn't a drunk or anything but he was big, black and he mistreated my mother. They both had a horrible diet of grease, grease, and more grease. I remember one day he attempted to kick my mother. I didn't realize he was not only sick, but also somewhat delirious. He wasn't in full cognizance of everything going on around him. I'm so glad that I didn't slap the shit out of him because he was out of his mind.

I told him, "You'll lose that goddamn leg the next time you raise it to my mother."

He kept this ragged-ass pistol around the house. "I'll make you eat that gun piece by piece," I told him.

In 1984, Alex became very sick and on Christmas Eve prepared a somewhat last supper. The food looked of death. It's amazing how people have that sixth sense of impending doom and death. He knew he was going to die He prepared turkey, dressing, rice, and gravy. The turkey and dressing were ashy gray. We did not eat it, period. Later that night he died.

Momma was alone again in the house but faired well. I would always stop by to see how she was doing and what errands I could run for her. She was still very partial to me. One spring day in 1985 Eunice was fixing momma's hair. All of a sudden momma's speech slurred and she attempted to raise her left arm. She couldn't do it. She became confused and frustrated. She tried to lift her left arm by using her right hand. Her left side was completely paralyzed. She pounded on her arm; her efforts were useless. Momma's face became partially paralyzed and Eunice knew that momma was having a stroke.

I raced over. Momma tried hard to talk but her words were mumbled and incoherent. I knew we had to get her to the hospital quick. I believe until this day that major damage had been done by not calling the paramedics immediately or getting her to the hospital faster. After momma's release from the hospital, she was in a wheelchair. We tried to arrange a schedule so that she had attention at least twelve hours a day.

To my dismay and utter shock, none of my sisters wanted anything to do with their mother. Each of them echoed the same reason, "I don't have time." I couldn't believe it. I absolutely could not believe my ears. It literally tore me apart that one's own mother could be so easily discarded without any concern whatsoever for her well-being. I found myself spending hours with my mother, then, going into a back room to hide the tears. I tried to hide it and put on a cheerful face, but momma knew. A mother knows when something's wrong with her child. After all, she was the one famous for putting on cheerful faces when the times were so hard those early years. And she tried again that day. I had never felt this bad in my entire life and I couldn't hold back the tears.

The most embarrassing thing I've ever done was to take my mother to the bathroom and wait outside the door until she had finished. It was by far the most humiliating thing that I'd ever done. Weeks later, caseworkers from the Department of Social Services began stopping by to take care of her personal needs.

God had shown up once again because I didn't know how long I could endure the sadness and humiliation that I faced every time I went to my mother's. I'm sure God was talking to me, telling me to correct my insane life and to cling to Him.

First, it was my little boy in the terrible car accident, and now my mother desperately needed me. There was no doubt in my mind that I needed to stop the drugs but I just didn't know how or where to find help. The addiction was too overpowering. Eventually, my sisters would come by and sit with momma for a while and things became a little easier for all of us. I stopped by as much as possible. She enjoyed my visits; I was still her hero.

I had started working at this delivery Company in 1981 and was the dispatcher. I worked the first shift for a few years and eventually wound up on the second shift which worked well for me. I could use drugs more easily because my lunch break was at six or six thirty.

Gloria and Eugene were living in New York and decided that Gloria would have Power of Attorney and move momma to New York with them. My sister also decided that she was entitled to everything including the house, all of the contents and the car. She arranged to move everything—momma's antiques, furniture and the car to New York. The strangest thing happened. On the way to New York, the truck attempted to go under a bridge that was too low on one of the Parkways. All of the furniture, including the truck, was destroyed.

Was this an omen? In retrospect, It actually worked out because there was no place to put the furniture other than storage. After the settlement, those of us in Charlotte decided that we deserved some of the settlement as well. After all, momma had four children not one. This resulted in—you guessed it—a fight and eventual lawsuit. It was resolved and life went on.

This obviously created hard feelings for a while, but eventually everyone got back on board. In the meantime, momma didn't receive the kind of care that I had hoped for in New York. Over the years my mother's appearance deteriorated. She had extremely dark circles under her eyes. Her blood pressure was horribly high. Her teeth and gums were in terrible shape and she developed a bad case of gingivitis. She eventually had to be hospitalized because the infection had spread to her brain.

I made many trips to New York to check on my mother and was always sadder when I left than when I arrived. I was smoking cocaine to ease the pain. I simply couldn't cope. Whenever she saw me coming through the door or heard my voice in Gloria's living room, she would try so hard to talk. She would be elated and so happy because, to her, I was her savior and the son that she had always depended upon. She just knew in her heart that I had come to take her back home. When I left, she was like a child whose parents had left them. I always felt so guilty because I felt that, as the only son, it was my responsibility to take care of momma.

The emotions were tearing me apart. I was being pulled back and forth, left and right; it was a crazy whirlwind of feelings and confusion. There were times after I used drugs that I truly thought I was losing my mind. I couldn't stop no matter how hard I tried.

Momma eventually wound up at the Hempstead General Hospital on Long Island. Her health deteriorated very quickly. She could only stare at the ceiling with a glassy look in her eyes. I couldn't stop the tears; it pained me so much to see my momma dying. When I went out to the hospital for the last time, momma saw me coming and almost sat up in her bed. She just knew that I was coming to take her home. It was too much for me and so painful. Being strong for her was the hardest thing I've ever done in my entire life.

Recounting these episodes now brings back vivid memories and emotions like it was yesterday. My eyes are welled-up this very moment. My momma never should have reached this point of neglect and abuse. I felt worse than I'd ever felt in my life. I never should have allowed her to leave Charlotte. I was the one responsible for her because I was the only son. She should have received proper attention. I honestly felt that there were resentments from the past from my sister that she didn't give momma better care.

That night I decided to go with my niece's boyfriend to South Jamaica in the Bronx. This was the most dangerous neighborhood I had ever been in, period. Driving in, there were guys in trench coats who were heavily armed with Mac 10s. They were lookouts for this notorious drug house. I knew that I had no business there. We were searched upon entering. It was too late to back out because Ronnie was driving. They knew Ronnie well so we went in and had a seat. Women there were servicing men in front of everyone doing every sex act in the book. These were hardcore crack heads and freaks.

I was very nervous, as Ronnie and his partner could tell.

"Relax, we're safe," Ronnie told me.

This guy bought out the largest rocks I'd ever seen. They were yellow. He had this large bowl and used a small blowtorch. Ronnie hit it first; then it was passed to me. This was unlike anything that I had seen or experienced at home. I was definitely afraid of this stuff and remembered the tales that I had heard about people using all kinds of chemicals to make these rocks bigger and more dangerous. All the same, I tried it. This stuff was powerful. I coughed and immediately went to an extreme high. After getting back to Roosevelt, I tried to go to sleep. That wasn't going to happen, coke doesn't let you sleep.

I realized that I was killing myself with drugs. I had major weird dreams and tossed and turned the entire night. The next day I was scheduled for a night flight out of La Guardia. It was the worst flight I had ever experienced. The pilot did a magnificent job and there was no turbulence but it was miserable for me because my sinuses were clogged and I had to breathe out of my mouth the entire flight back. I was miserable.

The next evening I was at work and received a call from New York. The manager took the call and pulled me into an office to tell me the news.

Chapter Fourteen - Death Was Not Kind

My mother died Halloween Eve in the evening. She struggled hard for breath; she didn't want to die. My mother was a fighter who wanted to live. I felt such guilt and wept most of the night. My faithful Emma was there for me. Now there were no parents left, I felt so empty without them regardless of my drug usage. Momma was shipped back to Charlotte and we planned the funeral services. I remember going to the funeral home after momma had been prepared. One of my sisters had to do her hair. They were talking about how pretty she looked; I thought they were crazy as hell.

My mother looked terrible. They were smiling and talking. I was fighting the tears and they were asking me, "What's wrong with you lil bro, what's wrong?" What a question.

I think they all had insurance on momma but money was the last thing on my mind. No one should have to die like my mother did in that lonely bed at Hempstead General in New York. We had the funeral, Gloria and her family went back to New York, and my Aunt Mildred went back to Kansas. I was even more depressed after momma died and the using escalated. Thank God I had the foresight to have the company deduct fifty percent of my paycheck for my retirement fund because as it was I was buying cocaine everyday. I really felt bad about spending my family's money on the demon.

I was trying to commit suicide on the installment plan. I realized that I couldn't stop and didn't know where to go or what to do to stop. I was alienating everyone including Emma. I wouldn't allow anyone to love me and I had simply forgotten how to love. So I prayed. "God, why won't you help me to stop? Why, God, Why?" I knew that the heart attack incident in that Greensboro motel could return; and this time it could be fatal.

Words can't describe the loneliness and alienation of addiction. There are, of course, many people to talk to, but the drug won't let you believe that. The key is knowing where to find them, arriving at a point of desperation, and reaching out for help. It's especially difficult for people that are financially secure and in a position of so-called success. I say "so-called" because true success is about peace and happiness that only comes from helping others and finding serenity in one's life.

My thinking had become more erratic and illogical. I didn't recognize the person that I was becoming. The mask that I wore was becoming fixated; I wore this artificial smile at all times. When asked how I was doing, I always responded, "great." But I felt terrible inside. I was becoming a shell of who I used to be. The communication between Emma and me was almost gone. The guilt and shame was indescribable—knowing that I was spending everything and going deeper in a financial hole, deeper every single day. I started losing eye contact with anyone that I spoke to, even my children. Emma and I were growing farther and farther apart and there was nothing that I could do about it.

Going from worse to jail

I was at home one evening in November when a loud knock came at the door. For some reason I knew that it wasn't friends of ours, or family. My suspicion was right. It was the sheriff's deputy. "Are you Thomas Saunders?" "Yes, I am." "I have a warrant for your arrest." I told him, "I'll come down to the Magistrates office the first thing tomorrow and take care of it." "Mr. Saunders," he said, "This is a warrant for your arrest and I have to take you in." I must have thought I could talk him into not taking me with him. I told Emma to call a bondsman to get me out. He told me before we left that the warrant was for back child support. I thought that I'd be out in a few hours and everything would be straightened out. I was wrong. I couldn't talk my way out of this one. The back child support amounted to right at $2,000.00. I was in jail for two weeks.

Emma had to call upon every resource in the book to get me out. They wanted the full amount in order to release me. I'll never forget the day that I got out; it was brutally cold and snow was forecasted. A few days later we were stone broke and of all things to happen the furnace stopped cold. This was one of the most brutal snowstorms that we had ever experienced in Charlotte. It would only be a matter of time before the house was too cold to stay in. Neither the buses nor cabs were running. Emma and I probably could have made a fire in the small fireplace but there was little Thomas and Levon, just babies. I didn't know how I was going to find some oil but I knew that I had to.

God was working in my life again. There is no way Johnnie's old truck that he called Bessie could have driven through that blizzard unless there was a Higher Power guiding it. It was almost as if angels didn't push that vehicle both ways. The real miracle was the fact that the store was open and they had oil.Normally, when a storm is predicted of this magnitude, people will buy every drop of oil in advance. I may have gotten the last five gallons. "Thank you, Father." "Johnny, my neighbor, had loaned me $5.00 and I got five gallons of oil. I thanked him from the bottom of my heart and knew that God had sent another Angel. As long as I live I'll never forget Johnny. I was a non-functioning husband, man, and human being just like my father during his addiction. Somehow I put together enough money to buy enough oil to last a month.

Three steps from the Blues

Until this day I'll never know how my wife tolerated me for almost eighteen years. I was a dope addict. I was out of work for at least a full year… at home… using drugs. The summer of the next year I mustered up the courage to start selling anything to create an existence for my family. I started selling roach powder door to door. Everyone laughed at me because it was blistering hot this particular summer. They laughed until the day I sold enough bottles in two hours to earn about two hundred dollars. The laughs turned to serious interest in how they could get started. I remember the saying. "He who laughs last laughs best." "I'm not hiring at this time; check back with me in a few months," I told them. I started selling this powder commercially and was developing quite a business. Obviously, the gorilla got wind of this and confronted me head on. "Doing pretty good, eh? I'm so proud of you; you're so smart. I knew you could do it," said the Gorilla. "Er... hmm... tell you what...it's time to celebrate and it's on me." In my mind I'm thinking, "HELL NO! NO! I'm not going any damn where." "Oh you're going for sure," said the fouled mouth gorilla. "You know we talked about you talking back, remember? You deserve it. Let's go to Mag's house. Now. Let's git to gittin... NOW!" I was powerless. I visited hell once more and continuously from that day forward. In the solitude of that bedroom after Emma had gone to work, I pleaded with God again. What I didn't realize was that I was serving the devil and had literally discarded the God of my father and my fathers' fathers. I was at the gate of idolatry. Drugs had become my god.

Becoming employable does NOT equal recovery

I started working at a transportation company in the early eighties and became a dispatcher. It provided a paycheck that was sorely needed to give my wife a break. We saved what money we could. We had already lived in and sold six or seven homes because of the transfers with UPS. It was time to buy another. Renting was and always will be a dead end. We had established decent credit and actually bought a home on Wilmore Drive for $5,000. The mortgage rules were different in the early eighties. A friend appraised the house, which he valued at $22,000. We submitted the appraisal for the loan and instead of the credit union loaning us the $5,000 that we requested, they loaned us 80% of the value, which was $17,500. We bought the home and put in a lot of sweat equity. We installed new appliances, central air, and carpeted the entire house. We refinished the solid oak staircase and the house was resurrected from the dead. It was beautiful. We had this fireplace in the master bedroom that was once a living room. The house was over 1825 square feet in size. In a matter of months the house appraised at $64,000.

I stayed with this company for fifteen years. I hated this job with a heated passion and got a good look at the system and society in general. But I was grateful to be there because it beat doing absolutely nothing. Racism here was the most blatant that I'd ever experienced anywhere. I had the majority of money taken from my paycheck and put into my 401K Plan. I took home very little because I never stopped using. The dealers could only get so much. I also hustled and sold dinners at work that I had cooked at home. This sometimes netted $25-30 a day.

I was doing a yard check when a supervisor told me to check a particular trailer. When I tried to unlock it, it had been rigged and the latch came loose and crashed into my face with thundering force. It's amazing that the latch didn't break every bone in my face. I had never experienced pain of that magnitude before in my life. My face swelled immediately, taking on a grotesque form.The pain was indescribable and immense. I couldn't see; my vision was blurred and distorted. The general operating manager couldn't have cared less. He told me to drive myself to the hospital. "I can't see. My head is hurting terribly," I told him "There's nobody I can spare," was the level of his concern. I drove myself to the hospital as best I could. I suffered a concussion and two permanent black eyes. I was now experiencing unparalleled hatred and racism first hand. Until this day, I know that somebody set that latch which was spring loaded, and I know for a fact exactly who it was. I was sent to the company's doctor, a plastic surgeon, for an analysis. This was like sending the fox into the hen house to make sure they're all safe. This doctor was the same as the two lawyers who fucked my son out of his money after being nearly killed in that horrendous accident. I learned more about the system the older I became. I found out that there are whites who don't want to treat blacks badly, but are forced to by companies and their demonic system. I came home one night and Emma was very angry with me. We went into the bedroom and made passionate love. I wanted so badly for our relationship to stay this way. This was the first time in a long time that I saw her smile.

After being at Wilmore Drive for a few years we were able to envision another house. This time it was in a very good area and we were the only blacks on the block. This area was in the South end of town off of Seneca and Park Road. Instead of joy and celebration, we wore the mask that we had worn for the last fourteen years. Thomas was older and Levon as well. People at church talked about what a beautiful family we were. I put up a good front and really gave a good impression to the outside .

At work, I was smoking crack in the bathroom, everything that I said I would never do, I was doing. Thomas had started to rebel against the father that was not there for him spiritually or mentally. My family was coming apart; we were separating at the seams. The arguments were increasing and the prospect of us staying a family was dimming. I would scream and yell at my little girl for squeezing the toothpaste the wrong way and all kinds of stupid things. I had become a madman and was close to becoming a lunatic.

My fears of hopelessness, uselessness, and powerlessness grew. I had lost all respect at home and for myself. I had become just like my father: full of shame, remorse, guilt, and degradation—only I was much worse. Everything that I had become was reflected in the eyes of my children. I was suspended at work for what I deemed frivolous and racist. However, looking at the entire episode in retrospect, I was forgetting everything and, in general, doing a poor job. I had failed at everything that I touched and attempted to do. I failed my two little girls with Mary, I failed my first marriage, I had failed at the best job I'd ever had and was working hard to fail at this marriage as well.

Emma would call home periodically to check on me. She could tell very accurately if I had been using by my voice. I was writing checks from our checking account knowing full well that the money wasn't there. I was so cunning and manipulative that even after Emma told the bank specifically not to honor checks written by me or for me, I devised a way to get what little money there was from the account. I would simply put on a shirt and tie and go to the bank. "You look great today," I'd tell the teller. "Your hairstyle is perfect; is that a new dress?" I'd tell them I had a board meeting in 20 minutes and that was all there was to it. Lies and manipulation were my new best friends.

I felt less than a man because I was crying so much in private and couldn't stop. I had never cried so much in my life, not even as a child. I stopped praying too.

The disease was telling me, "Don't you dare ask God for anything. You're too disgusting and worthless."

Self-pity is dangerous at any point in life. Add denial and you have a lethal weapon. I had this bullshit going through my head that real men don't cry, but I couldn't stop. Some addicts will cling to this denial until death rings their bell. The obituary never gives the cause of death. It doesn't say death by heart attack, massive stroke, or prolonged drug usage.

I was losing my mind. I left work one night in a fierce thunderstorm with lightning everywhere. The car, for some reason, stopped on I-77 going to Wilmore. I actually left the car on the highway and walked about a mile in this raging storm to cop some dope. I was soaking wet and being driven by a demonic force to get drugs at any cost. Nothing else mattered.

I was forgetting important things, my memory was slipping the more I used. I stayed constipated and my breath could peel paint. I could envision becoming a derelict and hanging on the corners but I would never accept that. Some of my worst memories were when I started at UPS, climbed the ladder, met Emma and we married. I say the worst memories because when I look in the mirror and see the face of disgust, disappointment, and worthlessness, I hated what I'd lost, and hated more what I'd become. I had opportunities: to be a regional manager with a dynamic company, a husband whose wife adored him, a loving supportive father, an attentive son. But I threw it all away.

What happened to the guy who always wanted to help and feed people? The guy that sent up such earnest prayers and was always the gentleman? What happened to the smart little boy who loved to play? I sometimes looked in the mirror and found that I couldn't smile appropriately no matter how hard I tried. I looked like someone who should have been institutionalized.

I have no idea how Emma tolerated me and my shit for so long. I guess she held out as long as she could and never gave up hope. I often wondered what manner of woman is this? The Saunders household was not a happy campground and it was all because of my insanity. I remembered the prayer in the chapel at the hospital when my son had the accident. I promised God I'd go where he wanted me to go and to do what he wanted me to do.

I wanted to fight this demon but I didn't know where to start. I was powerless over my addiction. I knew that I couldn't lose faith that one day I would stop using dope. If I lost hope, I might as well overdose and call it a day.

I simply could not go on living with me—the addict. I knew the numbers from trying to understand my father. Addicts hurt and harm a lot of people, but we harm ourselves the most. That's the reason the majority of us don't make it; we give up, lose hope, go insane, and die.

My journey to the end of the road

I made the decision to go to EAP, the employee assistance program at my job. I sat down and said, "I have a major problem and I need help."

That was probably the biggest and most important decision I've ever made in my entire life. I had to reach out for help, or perish. I couldn't go another step or another day living in the insanity that had consumed my life.

I made it to treatment for this demon of a disease. I stayed there on a thirty-day outpatient program. I was doing well, but as I got close to being clean for thirty days, the gorilla whispered to me.

"You've done good, real good. We need to celebrate. No hard stuff, just one little drink," he told me. "Thomas, I'm so proud of you, so is Emma. You can do just one because you're totally cured. See for yourself."

That would have been that if he had left it there, but he didn't. He would tell me at night in my sleep, and the next day…over…and over...just one more for old times sake.

"You deserve a little fun, you and Emma both."

I'm sure you know who won that discussion.

The company had a party for the employees, and, of course, liquor was involved. I'd been clean for thirty days and couldn't wait. I even convinced my wife that I would definitely be okay if I only had one. But if you know anything, you know there is no such thing as a social addict. One is too many and a thousand never enough. I had that one followed by two more.

Guilt set in immediately. I needed something stronger to drown it. I kissed my wife.

"I love you so much," I told her. "I'm a little nervous; I need something to calm me down. One joint from the block won't hurt me," I assured her.

We were both looking good and feeling good. After all, it was time to celebrate my having been clean for thirty days. She thought that I was getting a joint but I got a rock. I couldn't believe it. I worked so hard to stay clean these thirty days and I blew it. When we got home, I told her that I left something in the car. I rolled the car out of the driveway so as not to make any noise, started the car, and left going back to the hole. When I returned, Emma said to my little girl, "Watch your daddy. Make sure he doesn't go anywhere."

This has always been one of my biggest shames. It hurts me to think that my sleepy little girl was doing her best to stay awake to keep her daddy from leaving again. Somehow, someway I managed to stay in. It was one of the toughest fights the demon ever waged. That was May 18, 1991. That Sunday I woke up knowing that if I didn't win that I would lose my mind, die, or both.

Chapter Twenty - Recovery

I didn't use that Sunday. I went back to treatment to confess what I had done. They threatened to kick me out. I begged and they gave me a second chance. Later that week, we did an exercise of writing a letter to our fathers. I was chosen to read mine because I was considered the intellect who sat out on the veranda every morning reading the stock exchange. I was into day trading at that time and had some fleeting success. What I was really doing was isolating. I read the letter. "I love you, dad… wish you could be here with me again… I know how hard addiction must have been for you with no one to talk to..." At that point, I broke down and cried like a baby. I'm not talking about sniffling a little, and wiping my eyes, I'm talking about shoulder shaking tears. Completely boo-hooing. I understand very well where these emotions came from because I had denied myself thoughts of my father and mother. I was tired of crying, but I knew these emotions had been denied for decades.

It became quiet as a morgue in the room. Instantly, I had a sense of freedom that I had never in my life experienced before. I knew then there was hope for me. That hope lay in telling the truth. I left treatment. I was now on my own again. But I left with this truth: I was through with drugs. This was one of the most dangerous times of my life.

I got connected with a twelve-step program and went to meetings EVERYDAY. There would be no more excuses, I would either do it or die. God only gives us so many chances. I knew for a fact that I couldn't stay clean by myself, I had to have help. I had tried to stay clean on my own for thirty-two years and nothing worked.

I was still at the transportation company and before I knew it I had 38 days clean, then it became two months. The gorilla's voice was not so loud and strong; it was quieter. I was feeling better everyday. I opened up in meetings and started sharing with gut level honesty. I remember picking up my three-month chip and then six months. I was happier than I had been in a long time. I could laugh again, especially at myself.

My wife really didn't want to have anything to do with the sub. She felt so degraded and out of place around these strange looking people. Many of them were homeless, having come from shelters. In her mind, this was "my" problem; I had to deal with it. I tried hard to explain to her that the more she knew about this disease, the better we could communicate. One of the biggest requirements for a marriage to survive the horrors of addiction is that the spouse goes to a sister program of recovering addicts to learn about this disease, and how to support the mate's recovery. This didn't happen. I believe she thought that she had to give up an occasional beer or glass of wine. This definitely bought on resentments from her. She was of the majority opinion that all you have to do is to stop and go to church.

This wasn't necessarily true. However, the first thing a person does after learning that his or her child or spouse has an illness is read as much as possible to understand the life-threatening disease and how it's triggered. It should be the same way with addiction. This didn't happen with us. In fact, at our graduation, when asked the question, "How many of you believe that this is not a disease, and that an addict can simply quit if they're strong enough?" My wife was the only one who raised her hand.

My counselor told me, "You've got your work cut out."

I knew that all too well. My problems in no way ended when I got clean, they increased mainly because I could no longer reach for a fix. The atmosphere worsened at home. My son totally disrespected me and would say anything to me. I knew that I could not deal with this and stay clean. My wife accused me two or three times a week of using.

I understood. In her eyes, I was just a little too happy not to be using. She had no program to help her through my recovery. This phenomenon incensed me. I was clean and couldn't understand why my family couldn't see it. I committed the cardinal sin of recovery. I "expected" them to understand.

I went to my sponsor for help. Of all the people I had to select from, I chose Jim G. He was the greatest example of recovery that I had seen anywhere. I could not believe the transformation in his life. Full of tattoos and an ex biker, he was so caring, compassionate, and understanding he seemed to me a saint.

"You've got to change your way of thinking," he told me. "Keep your expectations low, your acceptance high." I must have done something right because soon, people with much more clean time than me were asking me to sponsor them. I couldn't believe it.

The verbal fights escalated between my son and me. I knew exactly what the problem was; he had a problem too. The night came when I really flew off the handle and one thing led to another. The police were called again. I was humiliated, shamed, and embarrassed. We were in the streets yelling at each other; it was awful. His mother supported his conduct through omission—that being doing or saying nothing. Especially when my son cursed me something awful in front of those policemen. The next day the police escorted me out of the house. I had six months clean and could not believe that I was told to leave my own home. I was in tears. I didn't have a clue where to go. All I was wearing was in a v-neck tee shirt on a cool day in November. I called my sponsor immediately because this is what we're told to do. This man came to me, gave me a bear hug, and got on his cell phone to find me a place to stay. I called my sisters and asked if I could stay with them for a few days. I was denied. I asked myself, "Don't they see how hard I'm trying?" I was literally homeless. I'll never forget that day as long as I live.

Even as my family abandoned me, God's kindness filled my life. My sponsor told me that I needed intensive care and he was going to make sure that I was not left alone. He knew that an addict alone was in trouble, especially during something as traumatic as this. I went to meetings and hung out with addicts as much as possible.

This guy taught me to really hug people. If they were like me, they needed it badly. At that time I could only focus on my pain and my hurt. I didn't think of the pain that Emma, Thomas and Levon were dealing with. The most painful experience of my life came when I tried to call home the same night to tell my son that I loved him and how sorry I was that things turned out this way. My son told me, "MF I'll kill you." I couldn't believe my ears and hung up the phone. Before I knew it, I was in a fetal position, sobbing for what seemed an eternity. It was as if my soul had been sliced in half with a razor and alcohol was poured inside. This was my precious little boy that I prayed so hard for after the accident. This was my little boy that I use to toss in the air to hear him squeal with delight. I cried like a baby, I couldn't stop. I was once again asking God to have mercy on me, to please forgive my son. The strangest thing happened. This incredible feeling of peace and warmth came over me that I had never experienced before. I almost felt the same as an infant suckling in his mother's arms. I felt totally protected and at peace.I have no doubt that God touched me that night because I've never felt that level of peace again.

When God wants your attention, he sometimes uses your children. When you start spilling your guts and telling the truth, real help becomes available. People would come to me after meetings and tell me how courageous I was to put it all out there. "I can't do it," they'd say. "Think of what people will say." I told them, "Do you care about people talking about you, or do you want to live?" They didn't realize yet that those same people they feared likely had the same problems. "You can't recover if you're a coward, you absolutely have to talk about what's going on inside you." I eventually moved back to Wilmore even though I felt the situation there was irreparable. At that time Wilmore was dope-infested and homicides were regular events. I was still clean-shaven and the dope dealers thought that I was the man. My home and car were shot into several times before they got the word that 'Tommy is not a Fed, he used to be my biggest customer.'

They also got the word that I was clean. There is honor among thieves. I gained their respect because I WAS clean. They definitely tried me, offering freebies as a gesture of friendship. One conversation went like this: "Yo, bro, you know where I can cop an eight ball? I'll hook you up if you help me cop. I wasn't in a friendly mood; I was sick of seeing the brothers killing brothers with that goddamn poison. I told him. "Hell no, nigger. Don't come at me with that bullshit; don't ever approach me again about dope unless you need a hole in you." "I didn't mean no harm bro," he said as he walked away. I knew he was an undercover cop and I was sending a message to the CPD.

Continuing the journey towards the light

Solitude made me stronger, committed to staying clean. I had a lot of time for me, and God. I stayed out of a relationship, mostly out of fear, for years. Today I realize I was in denial, still am. I never admitted to anyone how much I had been hurt. Perhaps I'll find a way to talk about that some day. One night I was happy for no apparent reason. I felt secure and connected to life and God. I felt resurrected from the dead. I had the most vivid dream of my entire life. I dreamed of men fishing at the sea. They were all bearded. A voice spoke of feeding the sheep. I felt compelled to start a food ministry to feed street people. At that time, I was attending Little Rock AME Zion Church. I spoke to the church secretary and asked about using the kitchen that weekend to prepare food for the homeless. "Other than the minister, please don't tell anyone," I asked her. She agreed to keep my secret. Ironically, a year had passed since I had been evicted from the house which was Thanksgiving. Using practically all the money I had, I purchased four twenty-pound turkeys, a case of cranberry sauce, dressing, green beans, rice, and rolls for two hundred people. I enlisted three of the brothers in the fellowship to help. We began cooking at 7:00AM. At the end of the day, we had delivered dinner to the most distressed and dope-infested areas of Charlotte. You should have been there to see these hard core addicts, elderly people, prostitutes and gang-bangers receive this love from brothers who themselves had been on those same corners. Grown men cried.

One woman asked, "Who paid for all this food," as she wiped her eyes. I told her, "A Jewish carpenter, he gave us the money". She responded, "Oh, tell him 'thank you', okay?" I understood what Christ meant when he said, "That which ye do unto the least of your brethren, ye do also unto me." I had planned this to be a one-shot event, but God had different plans. Every week for a full year, we were at the church on Saturday mornings cooking without fail. The guys left me one at a time. But an angel named Ann G stepped in with both feet and a host of volunteers. Ann was unfailing, unfaltering, and tireless. She and the other members walked the walk. Thanks to all of you. After one year, we had delivered 10,000 meals. Soon after that, I left the church, but Ann continued to this day feeding the sheep. I had peace and serenity in my life that surpassed human understanding. I was a totally different man mentally, spiritually, and physically. My credit score had even increased to around 715. I kept the house immaculate. I've always been a neat person and never forgot momma's Pine Sol from the Fairview Homes. I use it even today.

Chapter Twenty One - My Babies Came Home

I received a call telling me that my two little girls were in Charlotte and wanted to see me. I couldn't believe it. I saw Mary for the first time in over twenty years. My little girls were grown. They each had a child of their own. All I remember telling them at the time was, "I didn't abandon you. I didn't abandon you."Their mother affirmed this but I could still see their doubt and confusion. It was good to have them back in my life. In addition to celebrating holidays together, we had dinner at my house at least twice a month. We were a family again; it was a wonderful feeling. I had my girls, a son-in-law, and two grandchildren. I learned about Jerry, the man Mary and the kids lived with since they were infants. He raised them as his own and from all accounts was a good man. He died and Mary decided to move back South. All appeared to be going well but I let negativity enter our relationship. I was doing most of the calling. I felt a little alienated when I never received any holiday cards—not even for Father's Day. Maybe they thought that their real father was dead. I reached a point that I said to myself, "I'm going to see if they'll call me for a change." That was six years ago. Today I know how foolish that was. I'm their father, the adult, and should have taken full responsibility to let them know how much I loved and need them in my life. I lost them again. I've been trying to reestablish contact for years but their phone numbers have changed. Renee is now married and I don't know her new name. I'm totally resigned to finding my girls and grand kids—by any means necessary. I love them; they're blood of my blood and bones of my bones. I can live without cards or anything else just to see them, hug them, and to break bread together once again. Today, I know that it takes time to reestablish relationships. And patience. It was time for me to stop thinking of me and to consider their feelings and emotions. The meetings with fellow addicts helped me understand and accept the situation. All I could talk about was how badly I was treated. "You created every problem you have," my sponsor reminded me. He was right. I couldn't, or wouldn't accept personal responsibility. He told me to talk about how "I" felt because that's what recovery is all about. He wouldn't allow me to talk about Emma, or my son. I became stronger every day in these meetings and one day, realized the urge to use was gone. The dope dreams lasted a few years but that's all they were, dreams. It's natural for addicts to have dreams of using.

Loneliness sets in

That Christmas was the loneliest holiday that I've ever had because I was alone. There was no one in my life. I put up a few lights and stayed home as little as possible. I missed my family so much. It felt good talking to some of the addicts on the street, offering them encouragement. There were a lot of mixed emotions because I knew they would be walking all night long looking for just one more. I knew that they would face howling winds and freezing temperatures. I also knew that I couldn't stop them; the decision to stop the death march would have to come from them. When the weather was very cold, I'd take hot chocolate out to the sanitation men picking up the garbage. People don't realize what these small gestures mean to people who feel that no one gives a damn about them. Many wondered how I was staying clean. They didn't know my secret. I had enormous help. I could never have done it alone, and would never try to again. I used every chance to talk to the brothers and sisters on the corners to let them know who I was and how long I had been clean. "When you're ready," I told them, "I will help you in every way I can." I'd give them a bear hug just like my sponsor always gave me. Now, years later, they stop me on the street and remind me of what I said. I don't remember them sometime—I can't tell who they are anymore, but they remember me.

Addiction is the loneliest disease in the world untreated. There's no such thing as a happy addict who's not in a fellowship or a support group with other recovering addicts. The feelings of guilt, shame, remorse, and degradation are unparalleled. No one knows this better than the athletes, performers, or those in Hollywood. I lived in a fancy house for maybe three years and wanted to go back to the hood to be around my people. I moved to Tuckaseegee Road. My friends always asked me, "Why in the world are you moving from this beautiful house to Tuckaseegee? I don't understand!" "I want to be around my people. They need me and I need them." It defies rhyme or reason, I know, to leave an incredible neighborhood to move back to the hood. It was like deja-vu: drugs, siren, and crime all over again. I was soon housing recovering addicts right there where I lived. If caught using, there would be no discussion. I'd put them out even if it were ten degrees at two o'clock in the morning. If you give an addict an inch he'll take a mile. This is the only language hard core addicts understand: no nonsense, no excuses, no tears.

My clean time was accumulating and I was changing big time. I was alive, free, and happy. I still wasn't in a relationship but that was okay. The best dates that I've ever had were with God. We had a ball. He took me to an incredible meteor shower one night. The next weekend He showed me a spectacular sunset, woke me up early and gave me an encore with this grand sunrise. I started realizing how funny little children are. I had my own little fan club. Of course, I paid for their loyalty with cookies. There would sometimes be a knock while I watched the news. I knew it was a pee-wee because of the tiny, barely audible thumping on the door. I also knew that they wanted a cookie so I kept a good supply on hand. Their parents watched them until they left my door with their bounty. Life was becoming so much fun regardless of whether I was in a relationship or not. I woke up in the mornings with a clear mind, eager to greet the day.It wasn't easy by any stretch of the imagination. I had to become a brand new person living in a brand new world. When I saw old playmates, I would always be in a hurry, I would quickly greet them with, "How's everything, how's your mom, your Dad, the kids?

Good to see you, bye." I sounded like an auctioneer I was talking and moving so fast. I would not give them the time of day because the possibility was always there of them getting me dirty (high) before I got them clean. I treasured this new way of living and nothing came before it.

Sure, I met women by the dozens but sixty percent of them drank more than sociably, smoked, or did drugs. If they asked if I got high, I'd be gone quicker than waking up at a Klan rally. Let me clarify something. There is absolutely nothing wrong with drinking as long as it's sociable. Today I can handle a relationship with a woman who is a moderate drinker. Smoking is another issue. I could never deal with that from anyone.

It would be hypocritical for me to condemn people who drink just because I can't. Many people can have a couple of sociable drinks and stop. I can't. Someone would have to wheel me out of the bar if I tried. I can laugh at myself today but when I look back a few years there was nothing funny at all. Imagine keeping every dime you can earn. Now imagine giving every dime you earn to the dope dealer? Imagine dealers who weren't even old enough to vote telling grown men, me included, to "get in line and shut up if you want to be served."

Chapter Twenty Two - Feeling Better Day by Day

The program I attended was powerful. It forced me to deal with my past honestly. Man, some of the feelings that surfaced that first two years were not all good. I wondered who my former wife was with. I thought a thousand times about what my son had said to me that night that brought me to my knees and in that fetal position. I thought constantly about the pain that I had caused my family. I thought about my mother and father and how much I missed them both. I continued through prayer and meditation to increase my contact with God and thank him for the miracle. I hadn't used drugs in three years and six months. The loneliness continued because once you decide to change your entire life people look at you differently. Some think you're square. I remember taking this gorgeous sister out to lunch once. I dropped my head for a moment of grace before eating. This embarrassed her and I never heard from her again (thank God). All that drop-dead beauty disappeared immediately and I saw her clearly for who she really was. I also remember a date who ordered a cocktail and felt uneasy that I wouldn't join her. I've learned that rejection from others can be protection from God.

I've always loved the song by Etta James, "At Last (my love has come along)." I'm not like the apostle Paul; I want a union. I want a wife to spend the rest of my days with. I know that I'm ready to be loyal, faithful, devoted, and even obedient to one woman.

The program required more than working steps; it also required practicing spiritual principles in all of my affairs. I joined three fellowship committees. We went into the jails and prisons carrying the message, met with ministers, and started new meetings. We provided public information. We went into mental health facilities and treatment centers carrying the message. When I witnessed how some of these folk had lost their sanity due to drugs I realized how very fortunate I was as much as I had used. I had cookouts and invited the neighborhood cops to stop by for a burger. This maintains good relationships just in case some of the dope boys, or wanna-be-gangsters had some bright ideas.

It's funny but I never had trouble as long as I was clean. Early on in recovery I had to stay away from Hilton Head and New York City for years—they were BIG playgrounds with many playmates. I even stopped looking at professional sports with all the enticing beer commercials and the beautiful girls in the itty-bitty bikinis. I guess you wonder what this has to do with recovery and drugs?

I'll tell you. Because I loved beer, and on those sweltering hot summer days, the beer on those commercials was as cold and enticing as possible. We all know that sex sells. Advertisers have this fact down to an art. So, the question I had to answer was why go to a smoking contest when you're trying to quit? That's insanity.

The cleaner I stayed, the stronger I felt. I felt worthy of everything good and decent. I would not settle for less.

My sponsor once told me, "I've never seen a person with so much confidence when you walk into meetings, you look as though you own the entire city."

"What do you mean?" I asked.

"I've never met anyone with the confidence that you have."

I thought about that for a while and told him, "When you have the faith and the relationship that I have with God, that faith creates courage and with courage comes confidence."

I was active in Church, serving on the board of directors and both choirs. I had been a scoutmaster for three years. Regrettably, the sermons now all seemed so routine and familiar. In our meetings, we practiced unconditional love, acceptance, surrender, forgiveness and to care for the least of us. I am not here to reap criticism at any of the religious institutions but I've learned there's a vast difference between religion and spirituality. There are many good people in church but most of them know nothing about recovery so I couldn't talk to them about the specific challenge that I had. That's why every church should have meetings for alcoholics and addicts. Drugs and alcohol are two of the major issues facing families today. At the same time, it's not a good idea to go to the altar and identify yourself as an addict. This could bring out the helicopters, a SWAT team, and a whole mess of criticism.

I had never in my life laughed in my sleep but I did now. God and I were telling jokes to each other. Life was good—not because of money because I had none. We all know it's true that money can't buy happiness. I had found something more precious than gold. I had found the gift of life—I had found me. Rather than give every dime that I earned to the dope boys, I'd buy used air conditioners and give them to the elderly who were sweltering from summer heat. I'd buy Thanksgiving turkeys and give them to the elderly as well. As a servant of God, this was the least I could do.

I don't even think about the rest of my life; I focus on today just for today. Each year I would hear the horror stories of addicts with many years clean time dying from overdoses because they forgot who they were.

Sure, there were times when I was tired of being an addict, especially at some of the social events, reunions, and parties. It seemed that everyone was having such a good time whooping, hollering, and having a ball. This was how it was at momma's fish fries and that was where the journey began.

The effects of the alcohol were all around me. Faces sagged, speech slurred, and heads nodded. I knew exactly how those people would feel the next morning. The ones that I really admired were those who could have one or two drinks and tell everyone, "We had a great time everybody, good night."

The symptoms of addiction are obvious: repeated DUIs and DWIs. It should be an automatic assumption that continued arrest for these offenses means an addict is involved. Our government has given oil companies and other big businesses billions in tax cuts at the same time it reduced funding (or non-funding) of treatment centers and other public services. It took me decades to realize the saturation of evil in this society. It seems that we have become a kleptocratic society—everything is about money and how much you can steal. The only evil worse than watching a person suffer is denying that which would help make him well. For the most part, my life was becoming more stable everyday and I was utilizing pretty much all of my time in a productive fashion. I started day trading on the New York Stock Exchange. I made a bundle. Within one year, tech stocks fell quicker than a prom dress and I gave it all back. I learned a valuable lesson: when you reach a certain level, take some off the table. I also learned that day trading was simply a sophisticated form of gambling, which can also be very addictive. The years passed by quickly. So did the clean time. It was four, then five years, then, ten. Today I speak at workshops, conventions, and whenever else I'm asked to share my experience, strength, and hope. God has given me much. Sharing my experience is a small exchange by comparison. Of course, there is no compensation for this other than the great feeling of giving back what was so freely given to me. To whom much is given much is required. Addiction is rampant in many families, mine is no different. I realize that you get much better results talking to a tree than trying to convince anyone to change. An addict will only stop using when he's ready and makes the decision to stop.

Chapter Twenty Three - Journey to the Motherland

I journeyed to Africa with my associate Dr. Gyasi Foluke in 2002 to see the motherland in my search for truth. We were riding through the streets of Kumasi this particular day and there must have been thousands of street vendors selling their wares—everything from toothpaste to combs, to fresh fruits. I tasted the sweetest pineapple I've ever had. It was hot and this sister was sweating big time selling her products. She lifted her dress to wipe her brow and I was amazed at how white her slip was. I hate to admit that I had bought into the lies about filth and other propaganda about Africa. I saw first hand how clean my people are. The same lies propagated about them had been told about Black America. There were more Black African millionaires in Ghana than there are millionaires in all of North Carolina. These were very astute, independent businessmen. Islam allows a man more than one wife, but my brother, Ahlagi, told me divorce is almost nonexistent. America's divorce rate is around sixty percent. Their wives and children coexist. Whatever the husband buys for one wife, he buys for all. Their system works; ours don't.

Every American—black and white—should visit the Motherland. An elder told me while there, "If you want to see the face of God, come to Africa."While in Africa, we went to the devil's dungeon known as Elmina Castle. This was the most horrific domain I've ever entered. Evil's presence was there. This was where captured Africans were kept before being loaded onto the boat the Europeans named Jesus. That door was the gate of no return. Practically everyone who entered the Elmina Dungeon shed tears; a Dutch couple did not. They simply continued eating their food. I suspect most Americans, black and white, are unaware of the period in history known as the Trans Atlantic Voyage. You cannot know and not be changed. The voyage that turned vibrant men and women into chattel lasted many months. They were beaten regularly to destroy any semblance of will. To escape torture, men, women, and children would jump overboard to be eaten by sharks rather than face the torture and viciousness of a never-ending journey. My brothers and sisters were kept in these filthy, putrid quarters in the dungeons of this so-called castle. They were packed as tight as sardines in these hot dark cells. I can only imagine how they struggled to breathe sleeping in their own excrement and vomit. The average temperature in West Africa exceeds 94 degrees daily. The temperature in these airless dungeons exceeded 120 degrees. Steam came from their overheated bodies. Disease developed and the dead were dragged out and tossed overboard. Even today in 2006 the majority of whites are not willing as to even much offer so much as an "apology" for these satanic and demonic practices.

The women's quarters were worse. The stench of their monthly menses, mixed with their excrement and vomit, had to be unbearable. These evil, wicked Dutch who manned the dungeon would choose a woman, have her cleaned up and bought to his quarters to be brutally raped again and again. The capturers actually had church services above the dungeons. These were sick and twisted people who perpetrated these horrors. I often wondered what god they prayed to; it couldn't have been the God I know and serve. Africa was some of the most beautiful country I've ever seen. On our way to Elmina we passed funeral processions where the people customarily walked ten to fifteen miles to honor the dead, all dressed in black. The rolling hills of the countryside, the Cape, and villages were inspiring. Afranie, our hostess, took us to visit her high school alma mater. I was amazed that the children, even when on their lunch hour, studied vigorously. There was no time for play or idle talk; their heads were buried in books. In the classrooms, it was as quiet as a sanctuary.

Upon our return to Kumasi we happened upon a street festival, and what a joyous celebration of life it was. We danced with the Ashanti and the Akan, and ate grilled fresh goat on a skewer. The clothing made by the villagers was brilliant and among the most beautiful anywhere.

At the same time, signs of Americanization were everywhere: in the clothes they wore and the posters of their idols. Janet Jackson, Michael Jackson, and Boys to Men were hot in Ghana. Something else I found disturbing was the influence of other religions on this rich culture. The Roman Catholics were there, the Seventh Day Adventist, the Christians, the Presbyterians, and the Methodist as well. No matter which group, each brought with it a white Jesus with blue eyes and flowing blonde hair, a rendition of Michelangelo's cousin, a homosexual model in Rome. The Roman government sanctioned Michelangelo to paint the holy family on the ceiling of the Sistine Chapel. He told the authorities that he had no idea what the Holy family looked like. He was given specific directions and since his cousin was a model, he was used to portray Jesus the Christ. Since that time, the world—and worst of all, Black people, think that God is white. Consequently, people were trained through mass propaganda to worship those that fit this description. How tragic a lie and deceit at its finest hour. This portrait of Christ-God was slathered all over the continent from the east to the west, the south to the north. This portrait was on billboards, pick up trucks, buildings, poles, street signs and hung on people's walls. When the Christians came to Africa, the people had the land and the Christians had the Bibles. When the Christians left, the Africans had the Bibles and the Christians had stolen the land.

When we returned to Charlotte, NC, we had a major ice storm. Trees were down and electricity was off over broad areas of town. It was absolutely freezing and I had to spend the night with a friend who was so kind she gave up her bed. I insisted on the sofa but she was not having that. (Thanks Deborah I'll never forget you for that.) I had established a nonprofit that provided structured housing to addicts in recovery. The more I thought about Africa the more I realized how psychologically imprisoned Blacks are in this country. We have given up on the enormous struggle for equal and civil rights.

We have been hounded and traumatized so relentlessly that we go through life unfeeling and non-thinking about who we really are. Sometimes I wonder what it will take for Blacks to become so angry that we make a non-negotiable commitment to our children to fight till the death for a better way of life.

Three years after my first visit, my beloved daughter and I embarked on another journey to Africa. This time we journeyed to Kenya, East Africa. We met the Maasai, the fearless warriors, and spent much time there asking and learning about their culture and rituals. My heart filled with joy as I saw what used to be my little girl taking hundreds of photos and spending quality time with her father for the first time in our lives. Our last day there, we were driven to one of the largest slums in Africa called Kibera with a population of over 750,000 people. This was one of the most distressing sights I've ever witnessed in my entire life. It was painful to see how my brothers and sisters were living in these streets of mud when it rained and the sheet metal shacks that were almost joined together. I could only imagine the stench and the heat during the summers. While distressed by the sight, I was glad my child saw this, to see pain and suffering like no person should have to endure. This was a living example of how those who have mistreat and abuse those who have not. How the wealthy turn their backs on suffering and fight to protect their stolen luxuries.

Our last night in Nairobi, we were treated to dinner at the world famous Carnivore restaurant. I wondered why they called it the Carnivore, and would soon find out. When you enter this place you walk around a grill as big as an 8x10 room with six men manning it. They were grilling zebra, ostrich, crocodile, beef, and chicken. There was no way I was eating zebra or crocodile, but after Lee tried it she assured me that it was very good. I followed suit and to my surprise this meat was off the hook. The cooked meat was red as an apple, it looked raw, but it was delicious.

Neither Lee, nor I would forget this trip for the rest of our lives. This was the most time we had ever spent together, and it was wonderful. She took so many photos that she posted them on the internet at www.webshots.com/LSaunders. I had a chance to talk with her about her, our relationship, and me. I truly regret that my son wasn't there with us.

I guess we'll never know whether addiction is hereditary or genetically linked. It will probably always remain one of the great medical mysteries—as are many other chronic ailments. It's not as important how we got it as it is how to correct or arrest it. There is no doubt that I was touched by the Master's hand and had divine intervention. I could have been a statistic with an epitaph and obituary long ago. I prayed to God to help me to stop the cycle in the Saunders family so that maybe my children and my grandchildren wouldn't suffer this extremely possessive and destructive disease.

My eight-year-old son has never seen his father with any form of alcoholic drink and knows that I don't smoke. It's very painful to see friends and associates killing themselves daily and me being helpless to stop them. I attend funerals far too frequently and it seems to increase the older I get. I can only pray for them and hopefully divine intervention someday, someway, will cause them to reach out for help. There is no cure for addiction, it is a chronic, progressive and fatal disease if left untreated; people simply don't believe it. In reality, it's committing suicide on the lay away plan.

Chapter Twenty Four - Racism and It's Association with Addiction

The reason is very simple, they wear pants because they're being forced to be the mother and father in these single parent households. Regardless if the men accept it or not, like it or not or believe it or not, the women in black society are killing themselves rearing children, paying bills working from dawn to dusk, platting hair, taking sons to the barber shop, dealing with thieving mechanics, creditors, teachers, PTAs, repairing things around the house, cooking, checking homework and doing absolutely everything that has always been designed for two. In some cases it's a break to go to work. This has been increasing now for decades as the men and women Black and white are becoming addicted in higher numbers daily. As the self esteem and dignity are being lost to this disease so has the oneness with God known as dignity. I often see commercials on TV that are degrading to Blacks whereas the Black woman is portrayed as domineering and angry. I'm referring to this one commercial in particular (Advil) where the people are at the pharmacy counter recieving instructions from the pharmacy as to where the Advil is. The white woman says sweetly aisle 7 then there"s the Black couple. She tells the husband "now tell the man what's wrong, he then proceeds and the pharmacist says aisle 7. She then yanks him and says "C'mon" dominantly while yanking him. It's all about portraying Black women as heavy and dominant. The tragedy is that most Blacks laugh as well while whites assure themselves that this stereotypical view held by them is accurate.

I wonder how many people have given thought as to "why" she's angry. I have and it's all about the God awful weight she's been forced to carry on her shoulders everyday for the past four hundred years. The total indigities that she sees on TV everyday from the rappers as well as her workplace. If she doesn't see the women shaking their asses on BET, she can't avoid the total alienation, disenfranchisement and treatment in general that she receives from society. She then has to tolerate a mate in some cases when he's there who abuses her to the point of physical violence. Let me re phrase that statement about she has to tolerate, it should state that she "chooses to"tolerate it.

The rappers refer to my beautiful, strong and Godly sisters as Hoes and bitches, I wonder how many of them have given thought to the fact that their mothers, sisters and daughters are women. Are they Hoes, bitches and sluts as well ? I can honestly say that some of our Black men have lost their damn minds. Be not dismayed my sisters, I'm here to tell you that you are Gods' greatest creation with all of your splendor, charm and magnificence. All behaviourist agree that poverty, overcrowding, dehuminzation and intentional mis education are contributors to feelings of worthlessness, low self esteem and crime. Our race has been experiencing this for centuries in this European system of blatant racism. There are many factors that contribute to some Black men being incapable of functioning as normal and average. These are some reasons that I believe contribute to the problem of addiction.

This is not a broad stroke of the brush insinuating that most Black men suffer from the disease of addiction. Nothing could be farther from the truth. It is however a statement saying that "every" Black person in Amerikkka suffers from trauma (emotional and spiritually) that comes with experiencing WUBIA- Waking up Black in America. There are successful Blacks in this society who have climbed the corporate ladder only to realize "this far and no farther." The real shame is that some of them had to denigrate their own people in order to do so.

You will subscribe to the European Ideology and policies or else you'll stay in the warehouse and supervise the mop and broom patrol. Even during the days of slavery, the Black woman had to bear children and be back under the blazing sun a few days later. She's never stopped this routine and has never been afforded the luxury of a break. She even had to rear in most cases the children of the slave master. These very children that she nursed, suckled and nurtured from infancy would grow up to beat her sometimes mercilessly and spit in her face (these CHRISTIAN WHITE children). She had to be the strongest woman in the world to endure the treatment, the rapes, the emotional and spiritual anguish of bearing the slave masters children and to see her daughters raped in some cases in front of her.

She herself in some cases was raped in front of her own husband and children.

The real tragedy is that collectively no one has uttered a mumbling word in her defense not even Black men. There is no holiday or day of recognition honoring Black women and the only thing that has changed is that the cotton fields are now in Glass towers called offices. For the most part, they still clean, work in warehouses, drive trucks and do whatever's required to rear and feed their children. Unfortunately black men (no excuse) have borne the brunt of the dehumanization and degradation that has plagued us as a result of the aftermath of slavery.

Let there be no mistake about it, slavery still exist on an institutional level. The Black man has been denied until this day equal treatment and employment in all segments of society. When a man has been orientated and taught through violence and from the barrel of a gun to use the back door all of his life, it becomes a way of life. Even after they abolish the back door, he will create another in his mind. Blacks in this society have created back doors in every segment of life for hundreds of years, it will take much work and committement to turn this around. He has been imprisoned for profit in many cases.

Disproportionately, he is in jails and prisons, addicted, unemployed, totally disrespected and murdered by his fellow man, racist cops and society.

The Black troops fought bravely for a country that rewarded them when they came home by spitting on them, cursing them and lynching them. Here in Charlotte, NC (the so called Queen City) Blacks constitute roughly 26% of the population, we represent over 72% of the prison population. Black women are becoming addicted in greater numbers and frequencies than any other time in recorded history. This is happening all over the country. Still she rises and she's still standing.

She has worked and toiled under the scorching and brutal sun in the fields, seen her husband lynched and her children torn literally from her bowels. She has been brutalized by the demon and raped at will, her daughters have been raped in front of her and her sons beaten beyond recognition. She without a doubt is the strongest and most spiritual woman in the world. She absolutely has to be. She is the most beautiful creature that God ever formed. Her bronze and ebony skin was admired by Samson, Solomon, David and even the Pharoahs and great Kings of the Nile. She has sit in Royalty amongst some of the greatest Kings of all times and she's worn the crown as Queen of the Nile.

She has simply refused to die or quit and can bear twenty children at will. The Gods of ancient Greece have stood in awe of her and the very heavens adore her. This society is simply designed to destroy Blacks with their policies and laws. Remember that it was only a short while ago that we were banned "by law" to read or to learn anything. The grand children of these same lawmakers are still enacting similar laws today. We actually have to fight to maintain our voting rights. Those Blacks that call themselves conservatives (code word- racist) are acting in concert with the sons of the slavemasters and actually attempting to destroy their people and themselves.

This is all done for 30 pieces of silver, they are descendants of Judas Iscariots. I truly believe that there are Whites who know that the treatment we receive in this society is not only wrong but demonic, satanic and the manisfestation of pure evil. They want to help but don't know how. Thank God for you Michael Moore, Donna Lamb, Tim Wise, Morris Deese and others. These are my white brothers and sisters who have risked it all to tell the "truth". I can only imagine the rejection and scorn they have received from their families and others.

This is the basic reason that many Blacks believe wholeheartedly that some Whites don't have souls. How could the evil continue even until today with such vengeance? It takes an incredible amount of courage and comittement to take such a stand. The alcohol and drug addiction rate is much higher in our society than any other on the face of the planet. No one suffers worse from alcoholism than the Native Americans in the Dakotas and those in Alaska. We are reaching a despicable choice of either selling our souls (selling drugs) selling our influence in politics (politicians) for thirty pieces of silver or simply "if you can't beat them, join them".

We talk about this being equal opportunity for all (one nation under God with liberty and justice for all). We all know that this is the biggest lie ever written, believed or spoken. I realize the plight these sisters are facing and how discouraging, dissapointing and frustrating this must be. They have experienced incest from sick fathers and spousal abuse from sick spouses. In essence what they need to do is to find the largest magnum made and even the odds. It ain't no fun when the rabbit's got the gun.

Today they are being totally disrespected by the rappers who refer to them and their mothers as hoes and bitches and still they rise. The Black woman for the most part still greets each rising sun praising God, keeping the faith and singing hymns of his Glory. They still go to the santuary called the Church on Sunday mornings with their children in tow and have never lost hope and faith in God. Lesser men and women would have committed suicide ages ago. They still pray and pray much thanking God for another wretched day here in this hell called Amerikkka.

Confusion is the child of ignorance which breeds fear and anger. The first thing that must be gained is not vengeance, back child support (which understandably is badly needed) but EDUCATION and DIALOGUE. Read to better understand why some black man have been sheltered under their mother's and wife's skirt for ages and why they must both kick his ass out as far into the streets as possible. He must be forced to accept responsibilty and funtionability to exist in this society. It's your duty Black man to protect, shelter and feed your spouse and children by "any means necessary". I know that I was in that trap of satanism through drug addiction for over 30 years however in the past 40 years I have only been un employed for that 12 month period of reaching a final bottom. It doesn't MATTER if you have to get 3 paper routes , cut grass or wash cars. The hell with pride when your family's hungry and the utilities are out.

We as a race of people have been wearing these damn masks for so long that I say TAKE THEM OFF! I know beyond the shadow of a doubt why the men are losing their self esteem, their pride and dignity. NOTHING has changed in the last fifty five years except they've simply cleaned the damn water fountain, moved it to a new location and taken the signs down. I know why our women, my beautiful black sisters are becoming hopeless and losing all joy in their lives.

I also know why most of the preachers will always be popular preaching the same theology that Jesus is coming soon and when we all get to heaven. Earth has always been the white mans heaven and the Black mans hell. We are still looking for the comforter and the miracle of change. We want to believe that someday, someway the White man will change his hatred for us and allow us a semblance of fair play and equity in this society. Listen closely and carefully, are you listening? THAT WILL NEVER HAPPEN! NEVER!! I know why our women and men are so angry. That feeling of total helplessness, rejection, betrayal and powerlessness is overwhelming.

The politicians and most preachers collectively have sold us out and in fact some of them want to be accepted as white "I hope you're reading this Michael Jackson." They've learned to walk, talk and act white wanting so badly to be accepted. They've learned to condemn their own people because that pleases the massa. SICK SICK SICK!

This is referred to by Dr. Gyasi Foluke as the illusion of inclusion. If you're black and want to become wealthy in Amerikkka, attend one of the top ten universities,graduate with honors, write, and work against your own people and Corporate Amerikkka will love you for it. You will be elevated fast. Look at Condoleezer Rice, Armstrong Williams, Ward Connelly, Colin Powell and others who represent the most influential of our race.

The book of Hosea says "that my people perish from a lack of knowledge." LEARN YOUR HISTORY BLACK PEOPLE! We are the Greatest Race of People that Ever walked the earth. WE ARE THE ORIGINAL MAN! Why do you think this designated area of Kemet (Egypt) is called the Valley of the Kings because Blacks were the original royalty and Kings of the earth. We are the original man and the original mother of all mankind was a beloved Black woman.

We must learn so that we can teach our children. Why do you think that those plantation owners and politicians passed legislation making it illegal for any Black to learn anything ? They knew that knowledge is power and power enables people to aquire what they need as a society, for their children and families. Stop reading that garbage " Hot nights and sweaty bodies". It prevents us from having not just healthy and spiritual relationships but to stop growing spiritually as well.

There is absolutely nothing smart about spending every damn dime we have on bling-bling and buying clothes with some racist's name on it. Buy a BOOK, SAVE A DOLLAR and TEACH YOUR CHILDREN WELL. The only thing that our children have been taught in this European system is that we came here on a damn boat to serve and worship white people. We need meaningful dialogue for those afficted with HIV, alcoholism, drugs, mental disorders etc. We need men of valor and who place people THEIR PEOPLE ahead of money, property and prestige.

We are all of God's beloved children. The Honorable Elijah Muhammad said back in the fifties that "we are taking on the ways of the oppressor". Look at the blue and green contact lenses, the blond hair and kids trying to talk like a valley girl. Our greatest loss is and always will be our loss of identity. We simply don't know who we are. There is an effort taking place to sue the state of North Carolina so that our children can and will be taught African History in the public schools. If James Loewen "Lies My teacher told me" did it in Mississippi, we can do it here in North Craolina.

This is not about Black American History but about the Great Nile Valley Civilization. We as a race of people need to be taught about our greatness. Yes our men have been disproportionately infected with HIV (women too) we represent over 70% of the prison population and our unemployment rate is 6-7 times higher than whites. Our poverty rate is 5-6 times greater than whites. The mortgage Companies, banks, lending institutions, every business in this country and the neighborhood stores have traditionally charged blacks much higher rates than whites.

The Government has allowed them Executive Fiat or the liberty to do as they damn well please. There was always a universal code in effect to differentiate blacks from whites in every aspect of life here in AmeriKKKa. Insurance premiums are higher, healthcare much worse, mortgage rates, loan rates; you name it the whole system has always been rigged and always will be rigged. Food that is outdated and stale customarily even today taken from white stores and delivered to Black stores.

I think that my next book will be entitled "The Gulf War". This book will have nothing to do with the Desert Storm or so called Iraqi Freedom War rather the gulf that is getting wider daily between Black men and Black women. I have referred to The Village throughout this book, the loving caring and compassionate Village. The villagers today are killing each other, robbing each other and selling off their own people.

The Ultimate Evil is Racism

Dr. Frances Cress Welsing (a noted Washington, DC pyschologist) writes that the root cause of insanity is Racism. One man's hatred of himself and his inability to possess melanin in his skin. The Native Americans were herded onto reservations for containment and total separation from society. The African Americans after slavery were herded into planned developments correctly called ghettos.

The first law of racism is first to dehumanize it's victims and use propaganda and the media to attach every evil in the world to them. The next step is to brand them as illiterates, disease carriers, immoral and dangerous. Behaviorists write daily about these planned ghettos, overcrowding and the effects of racism. In cases today there are these Knee-gros who have sold their souls to the devil. These are the Judas Iscariots of today, the serpents and race traitors.

Harriette Tubman and Winnie Mandela would'nt have tolerated these vipers for ten minutes. They simply would have ended their miserable existence with a blast or neck lace to the head. I am NOT

A RACIST as a matter of fact one of my best friends on this planet is white. I hope that he's still my friend after this book. I love him more than a brother. I simply promised Yahway and his son Yeshua that I would praise him in spirit and in truth for the rest of my natural life and through eternity. Half truths will always total whole lies.

The problem is that silence is condoning and Ronald Reagan referred to this segment of society as the Silent Majority. It was Ronald Reagan that bought respectability back to racism. He actually encouraged them to continue their evil and sadistic policies as a society. When I think that the freedom fighters (Michael Schwerner, Andrew Goodman and James Chaney/these innocent lambs) were brutally beaten and killed in Philadelphia Mississippi and that of all the places in Amerikkka Ronald Reagan could have announced his presidency, he chose to announce it in Philadelphia Mississippi literally on the graves of these slaughtered children.

He was supported by so many which speaks volumes about this country's morals. The fact that these silent majority have said nothing about the lynchings, the Rodney Kings, the James Byrd Jrs, Emmett Tills and the other demonic and vicious assaults on Blacks in this country is a testament to where their hearts are. These acts have been sanctioned by the government and these so called religious zealots and churches now for over four hundred years.

We as a country asked the question on a documentary about a year ago "Why Do They Hate Us?" This was in reference to the slaughtering and bloodshed in the Middle East. It seems that an idiot would have more sense than to ask such an insane question. We could just as well ask the same question here in Amerikkka about Blacks. We have been burned alive, castrated, lynched, beheaded, beaten to death and drug by pick up trucks until our bodies were torn apart and yet we wonder why race relations are so horrible here in Amerikkka. There are those who believe that we should be "grateful" just to be here.

Collectively, the white community has the following statement about these atrocities "pass the rolls please" at the dinner table because "most" collectively have no concience, guilt or remorse for the terror that Blacks have suffered in this racist society, never have and never will. It will take a concerted effort to even start the process of any type of reconciliation. The majority of whites collectively will not so much as apologize for ANYTHING! We have compensated the Jews for something that happened in Germany, the Japanese for their internment, the Indigenous People for killing 60 million of them and stealing their land and the tobacco growers for producing the drug nicotine and addicting over 52,000,000 people in this country but as far as Blacks the belief is that "they don't deserve a dime" and are not going to get it.

It is also one of the most dangerous drugs known to man. We've compensated the hog farmers for polluting our waterways and streams yet they are not willing to give a nickel to a people who lost over 300 million souls in the trans Atlantic passage, from lynchings, from guns and by any means slaughtered (Read the Real Holocaust by Dr. Gyasi Foluke) We were killed for the simple pleasure of some whites and total evil and satanic beliefs. We were the most defenseless people other than the jews in the holocaust that have ever existed. We had to witness our wives being raped, our children brutally taken from us, we watched as our men were castrated, beheaded, disemboweled alive (intestines pulled from the body) and brutally burned screaming and writhing alive until death was merciful. I don't mean to incense anyone and have you think that all whites are the same because as we all know, they're not.

I thank God for those brave civil rights workers in Philadelphia Mississippi who were brutally murdered by these demons. They were fighting for Black people. God rest your souls Andrew Goodman, Michael Schwerner and James Chaney. You were all heroes and crusaders. There are whites who are fighting for us when we don't even fight for ourselves. Martin Luther King said "We will either live together as men or die together as fools." The Middle East is a wake up call that might doesn't make right. It's very distressing to think that less that a handful of rabid racist control power for literally the entire universe. However they couldn't control without being voted into office and with the full approval of the masses.

These people consider themselves Christians but don't have a clue about their own history of Christianity. It was the Christians who went to Africa with the bibles and taught this religion of worshiping this white Jesus. It was Micheangelo who painted his homosexual cousin who happened to be a model on the ceiling at the Sistine Chapel and called him Jesus Christ. His cousin had florentine features of blue eyes and blond hair, all of the attributes of a Mediteranean. Let there be no mistake about it, when the Christians left Africa after teaching "their" religion to the Africans, they took the land and left the Africans with the bibles. These Christians were very instrumental as were the Catholics in Slavery.

They have been just as much instrumental in some of the most horrific wars and bloodshed that history has known. Getting back to "Why women wear pants", my heart goes out to the sisters who feel abandoned, betrayed and abandoned. I know because I was one of those brothers that suffered from addiction and also a disease known as WUBIA waking up black in Amerikkka. I feel that the best solution and start at this point always has been and always will be dialogue. WE MUST TALK because if we don't talk, we'll use. Believe it or not these brothers feel just as bad maybe worse than the sisters because they don't understand what's wrong with them. They wear the mask everyday having to skin and grin for the massa on these plantations called jobs while wanting to literally die inside.

The Black male indeed is becoming extinct by a carefully orchestrated system of genocidal warfare that is being executed phycologically and systemically everyday in Amerikkka. It starts dramatically in pre school when our children become hostages in this cold and racist system. I think that intergration was the worst curse ever exacted upon the Black race. Intergration required our children to be handled by people who didn't like them, didn't understand them and who showed this vividly in their handling of them. They are being treated in most cases as convicts being prepared for the penal system. Dr. Gyasi Foluke speaks very succinctly about "the polyglot factor" in as much as Black children are unlike any race of children on this planet.

They must be handled and treated differently because of their memories of slavery, their treatment, their alienation and degradation on a daily basis in this society. Sadly, some of these teachers are Black who have been trained according to European standards and beliefs. They themselves don't have a clue about their rich and powerful history and culture. The teacher cannot teach what he has not learned. Dr Carter G Woodson succinctly states in "The Mis education of the Negro "that those Blacks who have attended and graduated from these top European Universities with honors are sadly in most cases those most useless to their people." They have aquired European beliefs and ideologies that are mostly against their own people.

It has to be stated to be understood the dire effects of poverty, single parent familes, hunger, community violence bred from poverty and everyday racism. The honorable Elijah Muhammad says that "Those that don't treat you right cannot be expected to teach you right." That makes all the sense in the world. Read Dr. James W Loewen's "Lies my teacher told me". Dr. Gyasi Foluke states in his "The Crisis and Challenge of Black Mis-education in America" would the Jews permit their children to be controlled or 'educated' by their collective Nazi enemies? I think not." We absolutely must start our own Freedom Schools to teach our children the truth, but we must first learn the truth ourselves.

We are amongst the most uneducated race of people in the world by "choice". Ignorance is not bliss, it's stupidity. Ignorance produces a weak people. People that are weak in stature and politically are always disrespected, circumscribed to the mop and broom society, alienated and rejected even by their own people. The first step of any journey is knowledge of knowing where one wants to go. There is an African proverb that states "If a man doesn't know where he's going, any road will take him there". The first step to realizing a dream is to first "wake up". Dr. Carter G Woodson's book "The mis-education of the Negro" explains why we fight each other, why there's no cohesion, why we dis respect each other and don't support each other. It's all about education and how we have been brainwashed all of our lives in these so called school systems all over Amerikkka. The problem is that whites have been taught this garbage as well. Here's what Michael Moore writes

Subject: White Frights'

This is an excerpt from the latest book from Michael Moore (the director of the critically-acclaimed 'Roger & Me', Farenheit 911 countless other documentaries) that is on the New York Times Best seller list: "White Frights" The article below, taken from the British Guardian, is exerpted from Michael Moore's new best-selling book (currently #1 on NY Times list), "Stupid White Men". Michael Moore Guardian Saturday March 30, 2002

I don't know what it is, but every time I see a white guy walking towards me, I tense up. My heart starts racing, and I immediately begin to look for an escape route and a means to defend myself. I kick myself for even being in this part of town after dark. Didn't I notice the suspicious gangs of white people lurking on every street corner, drinking Starbucks and wearing their gang colours of Gap turquoise or J Crew mauve? What an idiot! Now the white person is coming closer, closer - and then - whew! He walks by without harming me, and I breathe a sigh of relief. White people scare the crap out of me.

This may be hard for you to understand - considering that I am white - but then again, my colour gives me a certain insight. For instance, I find myself pretty scary a lot of the time, so I know what I'm talking about. You can take my word for it: if you find yourself suddenly surrounded by white people, you better watch out. Anything can happen. As white people, we've been lulled into thinking it's safe to be around other white people. We've been taught since birth that it's the people of that other colour we need to fear. They're the ones who'll slit your throat! Yet as I look back on my life, a strange but unmistakable pattern seems to emerge.

Every person who has ever harmed me in my lifetime - the boss who fired me, the teacher who flunked me, the principal who punished me, the kid who hit me in the eye with a rock, the executive who didn't renew TV Nation, the guy who was stalking me for three years, the accountant who double-paid my taxes, the drunk who smashed into me, the burglar who stole my stereo, the contractor who overcharged me, the girlfriend who left me, the next girlfriend who left even sooner, the person in the office who stole checks from my checkbook and wrote them out to himself for a total of $16,000 - every one of these individuals has been a white person.

Coincidence? I think not. I have never been attacked by a black person, never been evicted by a black person, never had my security deposit ripped off by a black landlord, never had a black landlord, never had a meeting at a Hollywood studio with a black executive in charge, never had a black person deny my child the college of her choice, never been puked on by a black teenager at a Motley Crue concert, never been pulled over by a black cop, never been sold a lemon by a black car salesman, never seen a black car salesman, never had a black person deny me a bank loan, and I've never heard a black person say, "We're going to eliminate 10,000 jobs here - have a nice day!"

I don't think that I'm the only white guy who can make these claims. Every mean word, every cruel act, every bit of pain and suffering in my life has had a Caucasian face attached to it. So, um, why is it exactly that I should be afraid of black people ? I look around at the world I live in - and, I hate to tell tales out of school, but it's not the African-Americans who have made this planet such a pitiful, scary place.

Recently, a headline on the front of the Science section of the New York Times asked 'Who Built The H-Bomb?' The article went on to discuss a dispute between the men who claim credit for making the first bomb. Frankly, I could have cared less - because I already know the only pertinent answer: "It was a white guy!" No black guy ever built or used a bomb designed to wipe out hordes of innocent people, whether in Oklahoma City, Columbine or Hiroshima. No, friends, it's always the white guy. Let's go to the tote board: *Who gave us the Black Plague? A white guy. *Who invented PBC, PVC, PBB, and a host of chemicals that are killing us? White guys. *Who has started every war America has been in? White men. *Who invented the punchcard ballot? A white man. *Whose idea was it to pollute the world with the internal combustion engine? Whitey, that's who. *The Holocaust?

That guy really gave white people a bad name. *The genocide of Native Americans? White man. *Slavery? Whitey! *US companies laid off more than 700,000 people in 2001. Who ordered the lay-offs? White CEOs.

You name the problem, the disease, the human suffering, or the abject misery visited upon millions, and I'll bet you 10 bucks I can put a white face on it faster than you can name the members of 'NSync. And yet, when I turn on the news each night, what do I see again and again? Black men alleged to be killing, raping, mugging, stabbing, gangbanging, looting, rioting, selling drugs, pimping, ho-ing, having too many babies, fatherless, motherless, Godless, penniless.

"The suspect is described as a black male... The suspect is described as a black male... "THE SUSPECT IS DESCRIBED AS A BLACK MALE..." No matter what city I'm in, the news is always the same, the suspect always the same unidentified black male. I'm in Atlanta tonight, and I swear the police sketch of the black male suspect on TV looks just like the black male suspect I saw on the news last night in Denver and the night before in LA.

In every sketch he's frowning, he's menacing - and he's wearing the same knit cap! Is it possible that it's the same black guy committing every crime in America? I believe we've become so used to this image of the black man as predator that we are forever ruined by this brainwashing. In my first film, 'Roger & Me', a white woman on social security clubs a rabbit to death so that she can sell him as "meat" instead of as a pet. I wish I had a nickel for every time in the past 10 years that someone has come up to me and told me how "horrified" they were when they saw that "poor little cute bunny" bonked on the head.

The scene, they say, made them physically sick. The Motion Picture Association of America gave 'Roger & Me' an R [18] rating in response to that rabbit killing. Teachers write to me and say they have to edit that part out of the film, if they want to show it to their students. But less than two minutes after the bunny lady does her deed, I included footage of a scene in which police in Flint, Michigan, shot a black man who was wearing a Superman cape and holding a plastic toy gun.

Not once - not ever has anyone said to me, "I can't believe you showed a black man being shot in your movie! How horrible! How disgusting! I couldn't sleep for weeks." After all, he was just a black man, not a cute, cuddly bunny. The ratings board saw bsolutely nothing wrong with that scene. Why? Because it's normal, natural. We've come so accustomed to seeing black men killed - in the movies and on the evening news - that we now accept it as standard operating procedure.

No big deal! That's what blacks do - kill and die. Ho-hum. Pass the butter. It's odd that, despite the fact that most crimes are committed by whites, black faces are usually attached to what we think of as "crime". Ask any white person who they fear might break into their home or harm them on the street and, if they're honest, they'll admit that the person they have in mind doesn't look much like them.

The imaginary criminal in their heads looks like Mookie or Hakim or Kareem, not little freckle-faced Jimmy. No matter how many times their fellow whites make it clear that the white man is the one to fear, it simply fails to register. Every time you turn on the TV to news of another school shooting, it's always a white kid who's conducting the massacre.

Every time they catch a serial killer, it's a crazy white guy. Every time a terrorist blows up a federal building, or a madman gets 400 people to drink Kool-Aid, or a Beach Boys songwriter casts a spell causing half a dozen nymphets to murder "all the piggies" in the Hollywood Hills, you know it's a member of the white race up to his old tricks. So why don't we run like hell when we see Whitey coming toward us? Why don't we ever greet the Caucasian job applicant with, "Gee, uh, I'm sorry, there aren't any positions available right now"? Why aren't we worried sick about our daughters marrying white guys?

And why isn't Congress trying to ban the scary and offensive lyrics of Johnny Cash ("I shot a man in Reno/just to watch him die"), the Dixie Chicks ("Earl had to die"), or Bruce Springsteen ("I killed everything in my path/I can't say that I'm sorry for the things that we done"). Why the focus on rap lyrics? Why doesn't the media print lyrics such as the following, and tell the truth? "I sold bottles of sorrow, then chose poems and novels" (Wu-Tang Clan); "People use yo' brain to gain" (Ice Cube); "A poor single mother on welfare... tell me how ya did it" (Tupac Shakur); "I'm trying to change my life, see I don't wanna die a sinner" (Master P).

African-Americans have been on the lowest rung of the economic ladder since the day they were dragged here in chains. Every other immigrant group has been able to advance from the bottom to the higher levels of our society. Even Native Americans, who are among the poorest of the poor, have fewer children living in poverty than African-Americans. You probably thought things had got better for blacks in this country.

After all, considering the advances we've made eliminating racism in our society, one would think our black citizens might have seen their standard of living rise. A survey published in the Washington Post in July 2001 showed that 40%-60% of white people thought the average black person had it as good or better than the average white person. Think again. According to a study conducted by the economists Richard Vedder, Lowell Gallaway and David C Clingaman, the average income for a black American is 61% less per year than the average white income.

That is the same percentage difference as it was in 1880. Not a damned thing has changed in more than 120 years. Want more proof ? Consider the following: Black heart attack patients are far less likely than whites to undergo cardiac catherisation, regardless of the race of their doctors. "Whites are five times more likely than blacks to receive emergency clot-busting treatment after suffering a stroke." "Black women are four times more likely than white women to die while giving birth."

"Black levels of unemployment have been roughly twice those of whites since 1954." So how have we white people been able to get away with this? Caucasian ingenuity! You see, we used to be real dumb. Like idiots, we wore our racism on our sleeve. We did really obvious things, like putting up signs on rest-room doors that said WHITES ONLY. We made black people sit at the back of the bus. We prevented them from attending our schools or living in our neighborhoods.

They got the crappiest jobs (those advertised for NEGROES ONLY), and we made it clear that, if you weren't white, you were going to be paid a lower wage. Well, this overt, over-the-top segregation got us into a heap of trouble. A bunch of uppity lawyers went to court.They pointed out that the 14th Amendment doesn't allow for anyone to be treated differently because of their race. Eventually, after a long procession of court losses, demonstrations and riots, we got the message: if you're going to be a successful racist, better find a way to do it with a smile on your face.

We even got magnanimous enough to say, "Sure, you can live here in our neighbourhood; your kids can go to our kids' school. Why the hell not ? We were just leaving, anyway." We smiled, gave black America a pat on the back - and then ran like the devil to the suburbs. At work, we whites still get the plum jobs, double the pay, and a seat in the front of the bus to happiness and success.

We've rigged the system from birth, guaranteeing that black people will go to the worst schools, thus preventing them from admission to the best colleges, and paving their way to a fulfilling life making our caffe lattes, servicing our BMWs, and picking up our trash. Oh, sure, a few slip by - but they pay an extra tariff for the privilege: the black doctor driving his BMW gets pulled over continually by the cops; the black Broadway actress can't get a cab after the standing ovation; the Black broker is the first to be laid off because of "seniority".

We whites really deserve some kind of genius award for this. We talk the talk of inclusion, we celebrate the birthday of Dr King, we frown upon racist jokes. We never fail to drop a mention of "my friend - he's black..." We make sure we put our lone black employee up at the front reception desk so we can say, "See - we don't discriminate. We hire black people." Yes, we are a very crafty, cagey race - and damn if we haven't got away with it!

I wonder how long we will have to live with the legacy of slavery. That's right. I brought it up. SLAVERY. You can almost hear the groans of white America whenever you bring up the fact that we still suffer from the impact of the slave system. Well, I'm sorry, but the roots of most of our social ills can be traced straight back to this sick chapter of our history.

African-Americans never got a chance to have the same fair start that the rest of us got. Their families were wilfully destroyed, their language and culture and religion stripped from them. Their poverty was institutionalized so that our cotton could get picked, our wars could be fought, our convenience stores could remain open all night.

The America we've come to know would never have come to pass if not for the millions of slaves who built it and created its booming economy - and for the millions of their descendants who do the same dirty work for whites today. It's not as if we're talking ancient Rome here.My grandfather was born just three years after the Civil War. That's right, my grandfather.

My great-uncle was born before the Civil War. And I'm only in my 40s. Sure, people in my family seem to marry late, but the truth remains: I'm just two generations from slave times. That, my friends, is not a "long time ago". In the vast breadth of human history, it was only yesterday. Until we realize that, and accept that we do have a responsibility to correct an immoral act that still has repercussions today, we will never remove the single greatest stain on the soul of our country. Michael Moore, 2002.

Thanks Mike not just for your honesty but your courage as well.

Tim Wise destroys the absolute lie of a master race in this article. It speaks of the absolute evil here in Amerikkka that has permeated the entire fabric of this society. Read the article below that addresses the pureness and Christian values of these racists that call themselves Christians.

Tim Wise writes

> I said this after Columbine and no one listened so I'll say it again, after the recent shooting in Santee, California: white people live in an utter state of self-delusion.
>
> I can think of no other way to say this, so here goes: white people need to pull our heads out of our collective ass. Two more white children are dead and thirteen are injured, and another "nice" community is scratching its blonde head, utterly perplexed at how a school shooting the likes of the one yesterday in Santee, California could happen.
>
> After all, as the Mayor of the town said in an interview with CNN: "We're a solid town, a good town, with good kids, a good church-going town…an All-American town." Yeah, well maybe that's the problem. I said this after Columbine and no one listened so I'll say it again: white people live in an utter state of self-delusion. We think danger is black, brown and poor, and if we can just move far enough away from "those people" in the cities we'll be safe.
>
> If we can just find an "all-American" town, life will be better, because "things like this just don't happen here." Well bullshit on that. In case you hadn't noticed, "here" is about the only place these kinds of things do happen. Oh sure, there is plenty of violence in urban communities and schools. But mass murder; wholesale slaughter; take-a-gun-and-see-how-many-you can-kill kinda craziness seems made for those safe places: the white suburbs or rural communities.
>
> And yet once again, we hear the FBI insist there is no "profile" of a school shooter. Come again? White boy after white boy after white boy, with very few exceptions to that

rule (and none in the mass shooting category), decides to use their classmates for target practice, and yet there is no profile? Imagine if all these killers had been black: would we still hesitate to put a racial face on the perpetrators? Doubtful.

Indeed, if any black child in America – especially in the mostly white suburbs of Littleton, or Santee – were to openly discuss their plans to murder fellow students, as happened both at Columbine and now Santana High, you can bet your ass that somebody would have turned them in, and the cops would have beat a path to their doorstep.

But when whites discuss their murderous intentions, our stereotypes of what danger looks like cause us to ignore it – they're just "talking" and won't really do anything. How many kids have to die before we rethink that nonsense? How many dazed and confused parents, Mayors and Sheriffs do we have to listen to, describing how "normal" and safe their community is, and how they just can't understand what went wrong?

I'll tell you what went wrong and it's not TV, rap music, video games or a lack of prayer in school. What went wrong is that white Americans decided to ignore dysfunction and violence when it only affected other communities, and thereby blinded themselves to the inevitable creeping of chaos which never remains isolated too long. What affects the urban "ghetto" today will be coming to a Wal-Mart near you tomorrow, and unless you address the emptiness, pain, isolation and lack of hope felt by children of color and the poor, then don't be shocked when the support systems aren't there for your kids either.

What went wrong is that we allowed ourselves to be lulled into a false sense of security by media representations of crime and violence that portray both as the province of those who are anything but white like us. We ignore the warning signs, because in our minds the warning signs don't live in our neighborhood, but across town, in that place where we lock our car doors on the rare occasion we have to drive there.

That false sense of security – the result of racist and classist stereotypes – then gets people killed. And still we act amazed. But listen up my fellow white Americans: your children are no better, no nicer, no more moral, no more decent than anyone else. Dysfunction is all around you, whether you choose to recognize it or not.

According to the Centers for Disease Control, and Department of Health and Human Services, it is your children, and not those of the urban ghetto, who are most likely to use drugs. That's right: white high school students are seven times more likely than blacks to have used cocaine; eight times more likely to have smoked crack; ten times more likely to have used LSD and seven times more likely to have used heroin.

In fact, there are more white high school students who have used crystal methamphetamine (the most addictive drug on the streets) than there are black students who smoke cigarettes. What's more, white youth ages 12-17 are more likely to sell drugs: 34% more likely, in fact than their black counterparts. And it is white youth who are twice as likely to binge drink, and nearly twice as likely as blacks to drive drunk.

And white males are twice as likely to bring a weapon to school as are black males. And yet I would bet a valued body part that there aren't 100 white people in Santee, California, or most any other "nice" community who have ever heard a single one of the statistics above. Even though they were collected by government agencies using these folks' tax money for the purpose.

Because the media doesn't report on white dysfunction A few years ago, U.S. News ran a story entitled: "A Shocking look at blacks and crime." Yet never have they or any other news outlet discussed the "shocking" whiteness of these shoot-em-ups. Indeed, every time media commentators discuss the similarities in these crimes they mention that the shooters were boys, they were loners, they got picked on, but never do they seem to notice a certain highly visible melanin deficiency.

Color-blind, I guess. White-blind is more like it, as I figure these folks would spot color mighty damn quick were some of it to stroll into their community. Santee's whiteness is so taken for granted by its residents that the Mayor, in that CNN interview, thought nothing of saying on the one hand that the town was 82 percent white, but on the other hand that "this is America." Well that isn't America, and it especially isn't California, where whites are only half of the population.

This is a town that is removed from America, and yet its Mayor thinks they are the normal ones – so much so that when asked about racial diversity, he replied that there weren't many of different "ethni-tis-tities." Not a word. Not even close. I'd like to think that after this one, people would wake up.

Take note. Rethink their stereotypes of who the dangerous ones are. But deep down, I know better. The folks hitting the snooze button on this none-too-subtle alarm are my own people, after all, and I know their blindness like the back of my hand. Tim Wise

Tim, I'm sure they conducted an intensive twenty four hour dragnet looking for some Black man, any Black man they could attach to these murders. I guess they couldn't find any. Incidentally Tim you do know that the media is owned by the same bigots and racists who are in George Bush' base. They broadcast daily about their fair and unbiased news reporting. What a lie, what a joke! Osei

*Life has a tendency to reveal it's hidden mysteries over time and man's created lies as well. The whole of the world has been taught that blacks are devoid of morals, disease carriers, illiterate and cursed by God. The entire world is now learning that blacks are indeed the most spiritual people on earth. They are the most forgiving people on earth and the most loving people there are. There was always a stigma attached to every race of man by some white men.

They called the Asians sneaky, can't be trusted, they called the Native Americans drunkards and shiftless. The Mexicans were lazy and the blacks were all of the above, illiterate, disease infested and had only 3/5 th of a soul. Normally when a person attempts to tear down another, it's because he's attempting to build himself up because of his many deficiences and defects. God's wrath is coming and his vengeance as well.

The absolute lies of racism are being revealed daily and we've learned in Iraq that might does'nt make right.

This Country has always taken life,property and rights of others through the barrel of guns. That day will soon end. As mentioned before God Almighty will tear the very face of this earth off as he declares that vengeance is his. I have never seen evil to the extent that it seems that this society as a whole has issued a contract for the death of God and his son who are one and the same.

I literally almost throw up when I see some of these so called evangelists on TV preaching to robots invoking the name of God and in total approval of the genocidal deaths of over a hundred thousand Iraqi women, babies and elders. There was one recently who encouraged the death of the president of Venezuela. This is customary for these people to kill, maim and destroy in the name of Jesus. IT'S SICKENING! The real tragedy is that there are Black robots who sit in these same congregations and are in agreement as well.

The Black woman has withstood it all, the tears, the humiliation, the degradation, the shame imposed by this society and total evil that has been perpetrated against her man, her children and herself. No other woman on the face of the earth could endure one tenth of this without committing suicide or going totally insane. Dr Francis Cress Welsing in her ISIS Papers states that "the root cause of mental illness is racism. "BLACK WOMAN, I worship the ground that you walk on and one day we will have a holiday that honors the woman known as the Nubian, the Queen of the Nile and the Virgin Mary. It took me a long time to realize that the Hope Diamond was not the greatest jewel ever discovered, it indeed was the Black Woman!

In the book known as the Metu Neter (Ra Un Nefer-1990), it plainly describes the two hemispheres of the brain. Scientist agree that the white race operates out of the left hemisphere and the Black race and people of color operate from the right hemishpere. These are diametrically opposed yet complementary functions. To understand this subject we must realize that underlying all mental activities are two sets of functions. One is in charge of relating us, and the variety of things in our environment to each other and to the whole. The other function is in charge of separating us and the variety of things in our environment from each other. In summary, let's note that the left hemisphere of the brain is in charge of noting the differences between things, separating wholes into parts, and enabling us to deal with sequential phenomena. This mode of thinking is popularly known as analytical,cartesian, serial, linear, deductive and last but most important SEGREGATIVE!

The right side is in charge of noting the similarities between things, and their relation to each other and the whole thus unifying them. this mode of thinking is generally known as the synthetical, holistic, congregative, etc. we must also note that the left side of the brain is extroverted and is therefore the means for the "outer culture" noted above. The right side is introverted and is the means for the "inner culture".

Simply put, the left side represents divisiveness, separatism and total difference while the right side represents unity, togetherness and harmony. Left side thinkers because of their extroverted beliefs contend that if you have enough money, property and prestige, this alone will solve any and all problems. They also believe with these one can rule "all" others. This is the primary belief for world domination.

Conversely, right side thinkers believing in unification, togetherness and that all healing comes from within. this has been the basic philosophy of Africans for ages. They tend to believe that all powers comes from God and our duty is to love and nurture each other. They also believe in the concept of sharing and divine intervention. The greatest belief is that we indeed are gods, though lesser Gods who have been given powers to heal and cure. It is also important to remember that Akhenaton was the first ruler in recorded history to believe in the concept of a monotheistic (one God) system of praise. This has been scientifically proven for decades and it explains why Blacks and whites are so diametrically different when it comes to thinking and beliefs.

Questions for you Black Man!

1. I know exactly how you feel after having been terrified and traumatized for centuries, the question is do you want your children to experience this and aren't you tired of your mate and your children living in this hell forever?
2. We both know that WE'VE been afraid of the white man for centuries but at some point we must stand up and take a stand for all of us. The cycle has to be broken, aren't you ready? Call on God to give you the courage to speak up.
3. Do you know why there are so many gang bangers and children revolting today?
4. Do you think that we as a people have abandoned our own children by keeping them in these school systems all over the country where they are taught daily about how worthless they are and taught by people who don't give a damn about them?
5. Why do you think that your mate seems to be angry some of the time (she's sick and tired of being demeaned at work, at home and in society in general)? She's also sick and tired of US not standing up for her and protecting her from the racists.
6. Why do you think your own children are angry most of the time? No one's fighting for them, that's why. Each day they have to go into these concentration camps also known as schools to face people who neither understand them, care for them and believe that they're incapable of learning. Unfortunately some of our own people are in this group as well.
7. Do you think that even God is ashamed of us for not fighting for our rights, our families and our very survival in this hostile nation?
8. Will you ever understand why we as Black people work like slaves all week and turn around and give every damn dime back to a system that uses our money to literally destroy us? Every penny goes back into the same system that has supported the likes of Strom Thurmond, Jesse Helms, George Wallace etc.

9. How's your dignity and self esteem holding up, it's shrinking every day right? (the end results could very well be drugs, alcohol and deteriorating health).
10. Do you understand why in x amount of years that the Black man could very well fade from existence?
11. Do you ever wonder why you vent all of your frustrations and anger on your wife and children?
12. Those of you that refuse to work and live off of some well meaning spouse, wife or mother should know that you're not worth the sweat from a dog's testicles. You should starve slowly and live on frozen ground under a bridge until you become self sufficient and willing to stand on your own feet as a man. That's about as spiritual as I can get.

The main purpose of this book is to convey that I love my people more than life and I'm prepared to give all that I have including life itself to become a part of the solution. What we have to understand is that NO MAN can harm me without God's permission. I can no longer go through life living in fear or being relegated to a less than animal style of existence. I even hope that there will be a few whites out there who can recognize and accept truth and become an instrument of peace and change in this incredible struggle.

The Black race has been traumatized for centuries and IT'S TIME TO TAKE A STAND especially with our Black men. The sisters are tired, bone tired of carrying us for over 400 years without rest. Why do you think they killed Martin, John, Edward, Medgar and Malcolm? They will always kill those strong leaders (Black & white) because they know that they have nothing to fear from the couch potatoes and drunks. We have spiritually died these past 45 years and all but a few have just sit down. I never wanted to believe what Minister Elijah Muhammad said 50 years ago that most white people are devils but history has proved and continues to support that statement. I will always refuse to believe it because we're "still" all Gods' children, like it or not.I know beyond the shadow of a doubt that there are indeed many good whites who want to help and become a part of the solution but they also realize that they have to "live"in this society. Also please remember there are whites who have given and risked their lives for this for the struggle.

Many of our people have turned to food, alcohol or drugs to fill the void of security in their lives especially when their spouses are missing in action. The first thing that happens when a Black gains prominence and wealth as an entertainer, sports figure or performer is that they're snatched up by some woman who looks nothing like him. Some of them have been trained since birth to always follow the money. By any means neccessary, go after the money by first marrying the money and having children by this money machine. When he acts up or gets out of line take everything he has including his socks. We've got the best lawyers who are very cunning and very powerful.

Don't be deceived my brothers and sisters, Malcolm asked the question "What do they call a Black PHD or millionaire? They call him a nigger". There are some of us if not many that suffer from "the illusion of inclusion" hoping one day to be included. My question to you my people is WHY? There is absolutely nothing like having been educated about your rich African History and clarity of thought so that we can see people for exactly who they are.

"I was watching Good Morning America Tuesday morning October 25, 2005 when they had a segment on titled Does your boss make you sick. They said that information from the medical community indicated that mean and callous bosses have the ability by creating stress and mild trauma to escalate blood pressure and create a plethora of other medical problems. I wonder why it took them a hundred years to figure that one out. How do they feel about Blacks who have lived with much greater stress and trauma induced 24-7-365 for well over four hundred years? This is an ailment known as waking up Black in America. This has to be a much more significant factor in hypertension (high blood pressure) than the salt issue."

Incidentally Blacks don't have the luxury of dealing for six to eight hours of this insanity five days a week. They deal with it every day of their natural lives. I wonder why they think Blacks face many more health related problems than whites? I feel that if others had to face one tenth of the problems Blacks face daily, there would be two -three hundred of them committing suicide daily. If Danny Glover can be profiled simply by hailing a cab in New York City and Oprah Winfrey can be locked out of Hermes, what do you think the average

Black faces from these Christians (Aryans) daily? Thank God for those whites who can no longer live with themselves knowing of the horrendous wrongs committed against Blacks daily and are speaking out and standing for fairness and justice though they stand alone.

I'll say it again, this book is NOT a blanket indictment or condemnation of all whites but it absolutely covers about 90% or better because their belief system is on one accord. I thank God for refusing me sleep until I involved myself totally and completely in this massive struggle. Some of those that continue to ignore it have acquired new best friends. The friends names are Smirnoff, the Johnnie Walker twins (Red and Black), Jack Daniels and Hiram Walker. It won't work! The only key to self fulfilment and definiteness of purpose is involvement and helping others. I hope this book in some way acts as a thorn in folks side and can only be removed by getting involved.

It's hard to believe that a middle aged Black woman named Rosa Parks stood up against the entire state of Alabama to espouse her beliefs. There are tens of millions of Blacks collectively who have not acquired that kind of courage in the past 400 years. Thank God for you Ms. Parks, may you rest in peace.

Head-On

The following chapter deals head-on with addiction. I talk about the different types of drugs, the symptoms, the ramifications and cost to society, the addict, and his family and loved ones. It's an earnest attempt to dispel some of the ignorance, mis-education, and beliefs about the disease. It should be a wake-up call to all who read it. Hopefully this will include the clergy, teachers, members of the judicial system and the political figures—some of whom battle this disease daily in private. Every sports figure, entertainer, and musician should read it carefully.

I dialogue with Dr. Dan Umanoff frequently and find him to be an expert in the field of addiction. The entire world should educate themselves on this fatal disease (untreated) by reading his book "Hypoism". He explains in detail after many years of research about this mysterious and deadly disease known as addiction. He has pretty much dedicated his life to the unraveling of this disease and seeks to enlighten those who in most cases don't have a clue about this baffling and powerful disease. In this article he explains the role of his webpage. He also has tried to reach those politicians who in some cases are thwarting research, treatment and funding for these programs until it knocks at their door and claims their child.

Chapter Twenty Five - Hypoism

Dan F. Umanoff, M.D.
941-929-0893
8779 Misty Creek Dr.
Sarasota, Florida 34241
umanoff@comcast.net

THE REASON FOR THIS WEB SITE

Every human is born with instincts. These instincts are regulated by a brain mechanism controlled by genes. These genes come in different forms called alleles. Different people are born with different forms. Some of these alleles are low (hypo) in activity. Low activity regulating genetic alleles turn out to be highly motivating and very low activity alleles cause addictions to drugs which are natural instinct regulating chemical neurotransmitter substitutes and the instinctive behaviors themselves - what I have named Hypoism. Understanding how these genetic alleles work and the brain system they work in leads to a rational approach to addiction prevention, recovery, and helpful public health policies. My book explains all this in detail.

Imagine you were born with a disease that would eventually kill you after causing you and your family years of suffering from a variety of damaging symptoms that both ruined your health and all areas of your life and you were told that you could not be treated until your symptoms had either already killed you or at least brought you to death's door with both feet on a banana peal – hitting bottom. Moreover, the only treatment available at that point is only about 20% effective or less, for those who get that far, only partially effective at that, and based on superstitious rituals! To add insult to injury you were also blamed and frequently punished for having caused all your symptoms and problems willfully, consciously, antisocially, and maliciously, and told you had to stop all this "self-destructive" behavior with your own willpower or be punished severely. Can you think of any disease that sounds like this one? You would probably say there is no disease that fits these characteristics and that no one would be so cruel as to deal with anyone having such a disease in this way.

Well, I estimate that 65 million people in this country alone with this kind of disease are actually handled this way and no more than a handful of them know they have such a disease. They don't know about this disease nor do they know that this disease could be diagnosed at birth and that once diagnosed they could begin a process of recovery that would PREVENT all its symptoms and problems. To add insult to injury they are also being kept from knowing about their disease by their government, all disease experts, treatment providers, specialists, the media, and even their own recovery programs who are all actually censoring any information about this disease from the public and are being told that instead they have very different kinds of reasons for their symptoms and problems, all caused by their own willful and self-destructive behavior and character deficiencies.

Is all this possible? It is not only possible but actually exists. The disease is called Hypoism. It causes all addictions and many other symptoms. It's genetic and in-born. See the list of addictions at bottom of the home page.

This web site is the only place where information can be obtained about this disease, its cause, prevention of its symptoms, its recovery, and what people can do about it personally and publicly. Besides the book, Hypoic's Handbook, that goes into the science behind this disease (and debunks all current incorrect theories about its symptoms), the brain mechanism altered by the genetics, and the delineation of the correct form of recovery based on this mechanism (not discussed on the web site because to understand the recovery one needs to understand the disease first), the web site also presents an organization, The National Association for the Advancement and Advocacy of Addicts, the N4A, where people with this disease can band together in their own interest. Use this information and let others know about it. Support the N4A, the only organization in existence today that primarily and solely advocates for people with this disease.

written with permission from Dan F. Umanoff MD

Hypoism
Dan F. Umanoff, M.D.
941-929-0893
8779 Misty Creek Dr.
Sarasota, Florida 34241
umanoff@comcast.net

THE MISTAKEN ROLE OF CHOICE IN ADDICTIONS, OR THE MORAL, RATHER THAN THE SCIENTIFIC, BASIS OF THE CURRENT ADDICTION THEORY, THE HIJACKED BRAIN HYPOTHESIS.

The major issue is no longer whether addictions, after the fact addictions, are genetically caused or not. The field agrees that once the drug is ingested, only people with the right genetics get addicted. This is the Hijacked Brain Hypothesis (HBH). This new thinking is a big step from the older theory specifying, absent any valid science, that anyone is capable of getting addicted because that theory said drugs cause addictions by the nature of the drug itself, irrespective of the user's brain or genetics. Some people still hold to this disproven biased belief. Of course, it took many many years to go from the old theory to the HBH. The critical issue in the HBH is its first sentence which says, "The drug is voluntarily (willful choice) ingested, then the drug changes the brain, in genetically predisposed people, to an addicted brain." Thus, the brain is hijacked by the drug despite the acceptance that only genetically susceptible people end up addicted.

So, currently, the field of addictions, medically and criminally, is run by the HBH which blames two things for addiction: 1. the addicting drug, and 2. the choice made by the genetically susceptible person to use the drug in the first place. Our country's drug policies are based on these two things; the drug war for #1, and the criminal justice system for #2. The best and most effective public drug policies would theoretically be based on the correct theory of addiction causation, an argument I will make later in this article, whatever that turns out to be, but assuredly it will never be based on an incorrect addiction causation theory. Therefore, if the HBH is incorrect in any of its statements, the entire theory is wrong, and it can't be used for public policy. Thus, if the first part of the HBH is wrong, that people who eventually end up addicted, got addicted because of a voluntary and free willed choice to use the drug in the first place, then the entire theory and all the policies subsequent to that wrong theory must be stopped.

Since even I, as well as all valid science, agree with the second half of the HBH, that only genetically susceptible people end up addicted, it's the first half, the "voluntary and free-willed choice" part of it that needs to be discussed and affirmed or denied via science, not philosophy. So, what is the science behind this part of the HBH? There is none. I can't even say that pseudoscience has been used to prove this statement. There's no proof, either using valid science or invalid pseudoscience, for the volitional use of addicting drugs leading to addiction. It has always been merely assumed, always, because it has always been assumed that all choices are voluntary and free-willed based. Thus, that initial use of drugs in future addicts is voluntary is a belief, not a fact. In fact, the most recent review of addiction causation, THE GENETICS OF ADDICTIONS: UNCOVERING THE GENES, Nature Reviews, Genetics, Vol. 6, July 2005, David Goldman, Gabor Oroszi and Francesca Ducci, uses the word "choice" five times without a single reference to how anyone has proven that free willed and conscious choice to use an addictive drug is in any way related to the causation of addictions. Everything else is dutifully referenced, as scientific reviews should be, except for this. Yet, they use the word choice in these ways in the article:

"The addictions are moderately to highly heritable, which is paradoxical because these disorders require use; a choice that is itself modulated by both genes and environment." "However, because addictions are in theory entirely preventable by law or individual choice..." "However, voluntary or enforced choice has met with partial success." "These moderate to high heritabilities are seemingly paradoxical: addiction depends initially on individual choice to use an addictive agent (so, if a person chooses to use a drug, how can addiction to the drug be heritable?)" "Furthermore, it is becoming clear that susceptibility to several complex diseases — coronary artery disease, obesity, cancer and AIDS — is genetically influenced, but also depends profoundly on lifestyle choices." The use of the word choice in these sentences is stated but not proven and not referenced, a scientific sin especially in an article from a peer reviewed journal. However, the frequency and manner of its use does hammer home for the reader the clear "fact" that choice is, according to this peer reviewed article in a prestigious journal, Nature, the critical issue in the addiction epidemic. Well, let's see.

The fact is that the valid science of addiction causation has shown over and over, in both human epidemiological and twin studies, and in animal studies, that what looks like a choice is actually not a choice but itself is caused by the genetic neurobiology that causes addictions from the get go. That's why Goldman et al, above, say, "These moderate to high heritabilities are seemingly paradoxical: addiction depends initially on individual choice to use an addictive agent (so, if a person chooses to use a drug, how can addiction to the drug be heritable?)" That's correct, it either won't be a choice or it won't be heritable. It can't be both. The paradox only exists if one believes that there is a conscious and free-willed choice involved. There is no paradox if the genetic neurobiology, the disease of Hypoism, causes the addictions as well as causing the "choice" of initial use of the addictive drug. And, this is [one of the things] what Goldman and the rest of the field has missed in its attempts to understand additions, this paradox. The fact is that there is no paradox, except within their biased and preconceived beliefs about addiction causation. It is only a "seeming" paradox if one BELIEVES the assumption, but not if one reads the science with an unbiased mind. Choice, as we use this word in everyday conversation, is no more involved in addictions than in homosexuality, race, or eye color.

Moreover, this thinking, my thinking, not their thinking, works as well for addictions where there is no drug involved, behavioral addictions such as sex, gambling, eating disorders, etc. Thus, from beginning to end the HBH is wrong in its theory to explain addictions; behavioral addictions have no causative drug but the people get addicted nonetheless.

Lastly, a recent paper, Genetic susceptibility to substance dependence, Molecular Psychiatry (2005) 10, 336–344, by N Hiroi and S Agatsuma, compares and contrasts the HBH, the plasticity model, with the genetic causation model, including the genetically determined "choice," and confirms that the HBH doesn't fit the science whereas the genetic causation model, from initiation of addictor use (initial "choice" to use) to addiction, does fit the science.

Thus, in terms of the word and the philosophical or moral use of the word "choice," there are two kinds of people in the world: 1. People, non-hypoics, without the genetic disease, Hypoism, that causes addictions. These people have a choice to use or not to use addictive drugs and don't get addicted to them no matter what, and, 2. People with the genetic disease that causes their addictions as well as their initial use of drugs, and other behavioral addictors, Hypoism. In other words, the seeming choice of initial use of addictors, drugs and behaviors, in these people, hypoics, is not a choice but actually part of the disease itself. They have no choice. Moreover, addictions are not diseases, as stated in the Goldman article, but are symptoms of the disease, Hypoism, that causes the addictions as well as the initial use of the addictor. Because Dr. Goldman and the entire addiction field are unamenable to this scientific reality, because of their unscientific bias, they are stuck in what he calls the paradox of heritability. But, there is no paradox because use of addictors by hypoics is not a choice but determined by the disease that causes the whole shebang, initial drug use and ultimate addiction. Goldman and the rest of the field of addictions who misuse the word choice and the HBH theory of addiction causation are deliberately misleading people about the cause of addictions because, in fact, they know they are wrong but push it anyway for the sake of the drug war and the government which pays them to maintain this untruth. Goldman and others from the NIH are the government funded hit men paid to maintain a wrong theory of addiction causation for the sole purpose of maintaining the drug war, the moral war against drugs and addicts. This is the biggest scientific and medical scandal of all time.

The Hypoism paradigm of addictions, the complete genetic hypothesis with its implications on prevention, treatment, and public policy, answers the "choice" issue and is available at: www.hypoism.com. The book that describes this paradigm is available there. My review article that goes through much of the science but little of the prevention, treatment, and public policy implications is at: http://www.nvo.com/hypoism/hypoismhypothesis/ The evolutionary reasons for why the genes that cause addictions are in the gene pool and how and where in the brain they work is at: http://www.nvo.com/hypoism/thehypoismaddictionhypothesis/

Now, you can ignore this argument and explanation and stick with the addiction field and Dr. Goldman, and help keep addictions where they are today, epidemic, or read my writings, let your readers and friends know about Hypoism, so all addicts and their families can use it to stop the epidemic currently maintained by the wrong theory of addiction causation, the HBH.

Aside:

To Decide: Verb, to arrive at a solution that ends uncertainty or dispute about which alternative to select.

To Choose: Verb, the act of selection between alternatives following a decision.

Choice: Noun, that which is selected from alternatives.

Thus, a choice involves a decision between alternatives and the action that manifests that choice. When someone uses the word choice this is what they mean. The critical caveat within this definition is that there are alternatives and that the decision is between relatively equal (free) alternatives, in other words that there are no preexisting constraints on the individual alternatives, and that there are actual alternatives, not just the appearance of alternatives.

Hypoism, the genetic disease, rules out any choices about addictor use and addictions for people with this disease. Thus, choice cannot be used when discussing addictions. If it is used it is used solely for moral purposes, not scientific.

The N4A, Inc.
Dan F. Umanoff, M.D. President and CEO
Re: Brain Chemistry Linked to Who Drinks
http://www.healthday.com/view.cfm?id=534744

The article states that Volkow says if high risk children of alcoholic families have high dopamine receptors they are protected from alcoholism. Now, that's a convoluted way to say that non-hypoics don't get addicted. Many people reading this email know what I mean by that but those who haven't read my book and articles on Hypoism don't. Hypoism is the genetic brain disease that causes addictions due to LOW activity alleles of genes like the dopamine receptor genes. So, these high risk kids weren't really high risk at all. They didn't have Hypoism so they didn't get addicted. This research is merely more proof that Hypoism is required for addictions to occur, something Volkow knows about because I gave a lecture on it at Brookhaven medical conference in 2000. Jack Wang invited me but Volkow didn't attend because she is biased against Hypoism and still wants to use words like alcoholism and theories like the Hijacked Brain Hypothesis, a wrong theory of addiction causation, proven wrong by this research. Volkow has done much work to prove Hypoism. Read: http://www.nvo.com/hypoism/hypoismhypothesis/ and check for her references. Despite this she still refuses to acknowledge Hypoism and has kept the field of addictions retarded because of this bias. Another author of this paper, Begleiter, also knows about Hypoism and privately told me I was preaching to the choir when I told him about it in the late 1990's but he too refused to acknowledge it as well as refused to let me collaborate with him in the COGA study to use his data bank to help prove Hypoism from that research work.

Until Hypoism is acknowledged and used as the consensus addiction causation paradigm no progress will be made in addiction prevention, recovery, and public policy. The problem is that the addiction field doesn't care if these implications ever occur. They just want to be in charge of addictions and addicts no matter how bad things get with addictions and for addicts and how bad things remain with the public consequences by addictions and addicts. The public needs to know about all this so they can demand a change in addiction leadership and theory so that positive changes can occur for the reduction of addictions and their consequences.

"Love is an action not a feeling.
Integrity is an action not a thought.
Anything less is too little." ---
Dan F. Umanoff, M.D.
Author of Hypoic's Handbook - The Hypoism Paradigm of Addiction.
http://www.hypoism.com
*President and founder of The National Association for the Advancement and Advocacy of Addicts, Inc. (N4A), a not-for-profit 501 (c) (3) organization of addicts for addicts offering free educational and legal services to discriminated against and abused addicts of all varieties, "substances" and "behavior*al," and their families.
http://www.nvo.com/hypoism/thenationalassociationfortheadvance mentandadvocacyofaddicts/
8779 Misty Creek Dr.
Sarasota, FL 34241
941-929-0893

In this article Dan Umanoff explains why he has the anger he does with those that make unfounded claims about this disease (based on ignorance) in which those claims can injure or in fact "kill" people with this deadly disease.

Alcohol and nicotine are the most common drugs used and abused. Alcohol is an intoxicant, that depresses the central nervous system and can lead to a temporary loss of control over physical and mental powers. The signs of drunkenness are well known: lack of coordination, slurred speech, blurred vision, and poor judgment. The amount of alcohol in liquor is measured by a "proof rating." For example, 45 percent pure alcohol would be 90-proof liquor. A twelve-ounce can of beer, four ounces of wine, and alone-shot glass of 100-proof liquor all contain the same amount of alcohol. In recent years, debate has raged over whether alcoholism is a sin or a sickness.

The Bible clearly labels drunkenness a sin (Deut. 21:20-21; 1 Cor. 6:9-10; Gal. 5:19-20), but that doesn't mitigate the growing physiological evidence that certain people's biochemistry makes them more prone to addiction. Some studies suggest that the body chemistry of alcoholics processes alcohol differently than that of non-alcoholics. Acetaldehyde is the intermediate by-product of alcohol metabolism, butte biochemistry of some people make it difficult to process acetaldehyde into acetate. Thus, acetaldehyde builds up in the body and begins to affect a person's brain chemistry. The chemicals produced, called isoquinolines, act very much like opiates and therefore contribute to alcoholism.

Other studies have tried to establish a connection between certain types of personalities and alcoholism. The general conclusion has been that there is no connection. But more recent studies seem to suggest some correlation between personality type and drug abuse. One personality type that seems to be at risk is the anti-social personality (ASP), who is often charming, manipulative, impulsive, and egocentric. ASPs make up 25 percent of the alcohol- and drug-abuse population, yet only comprise about 3 percent of the general population. The social costs of alcohol are staggering.

Alcoholism is the third largest health problem (following heart disease and cancer). There are an estimated 15-18 million problem drinkers in the American adult population and an estimated 4.3 million teenage problem drinkers. Half of all traffic fatalities and one-third of all traffic injuries are alcohol-related. Alcohol is involved in 67 percent of all murders and 33 percent of all suicides Alcohol is also a prime reason for the breakdown of the family. High percentages of family violence, parental abuse and neglect, lost wages, and divorce are tied to the abuse of alcohol in this country. In one poll on alcohol done for Christianity Today by George Gallup, nearly one-fourth of all Americans cited alcohol and/or drug abuse as one of the three reasons most responsible for the high divorce rate in this country.

Since the publication of Janet Geringer Woitiz's book Adult Children of Alcoholics, society has begun to understand the long-term effect of alcoholism on future generations. Children of Alcoholics (COAs) exhibit a number of traits including guessing what normal behavior is, having difficulty following a project from beginning to end, judging themselves without mercy, and having difficulty with intimate relationships. The toxic effects of alcohol are also well known: they often cause permanent damage to vital organs like the brain and the liver. Death occurs if alcohol is taken in large enough amounts. When the blood alcohol level reaches four-tenths of 1 percent, unconsciousness occurs; at five-tenths of 1 percent, alcohol poisoning and death occurs

Marijuana is produced from the hemp plant (Cannabis sativa), which grows well throughout the world. Marijuana has been considered a "gateway drug" because of its potential to lead young people to experiment with stronger drugs such as heroin and cocaine. In 1978, an alarming 10 percent of all high-school seniors smoked marijuana every day. Although that percentage has dropped significantly, officials still estimate that about one-third of all teenagers have tried marijuana. Marijuana is an intoxicant that is usually smoked in order to induce a feeling of euphoria lasting two to four hours. Physical effects include an increase in heart rate, bloodshot eyes, a dry mouth and throat, and increased appetite. Marijuana can impair or reduce short-term memory and comprehension. It can reduce one's ability to perform tasks requiring concentration (such as driving a car). Marijuana can also produce paranoia and psychosis. Because most marijuana users inhale unfiltered smoke and hold it in their lungs for as long as possible, it causes damage to the lungs and pulmonary system. Marijuana smoke also has more cancer-causing agents than tobacco smoke. Marijuana also interferes with the immune system and reduces the sperm count in males.

Cocaine occurs naturally in the leaves of coca plants and was reportedly chewed by natives in Peru as early as the sixth century. It became widely used in beverages (like Coca-Cola) and medicines in the nineteenth century but was restricted in 1914 by the Harrison Narcotics Act. Some experts estimate that more than 30 million Americans have tried cocaine. Government surveys suggest there may be as many as 6 million regular users. Every day some 5,000 neophytes sniff a line of coke for the first time. When the popularity of cocaine grew in the 1970s, most snorted cocaine and some dissolved the drug in water and injected it intravenously.

Today the government estimates more than 300,000 Americans are intravenous cocaine users. In recent years, snorting cocaine has given way to smoking it. Snorting cocaine limits the intensity of the effect because the blood vessels in the nose are constricted.

Smoking cocaine delivers a much more intense high. Smoke goes directly to the lungs and then to the heart. On the next heartbeat, it is on the way to the brain. Dr. Anna Rose Childress at the University of Pennsylvania notes that "you can become compulsively involved with snorted cocaine. We have many Hollywood movie stars without a nasal septum to prove that." But when cocaine is smoked "it seems to have incredibly powerful effects that tend to set up a compulsive addictive cycle more quickly than anything that we've seen."

Cocaine is a stimulant and increases heart rate, restricts blood vessels, and stimulates mental awareness. Users say it is an ego-builder. Along with increased energy comes a feeling of personal supremacy: the illusion of being smarter, sexier, and more competent than anyone else. But while the cocaine confidence makes users feel indestructible, the crash from cocaine leaves them depressed, paranoid, and searching for more. Until recently, people speaking of cocaine dependence never called it an addiction. Cocaine's withdrawal symptoms are not physically wrenching like those of heroin and alcohol. Yet cocaine involves compulsion, loss of control, and continued use in spite of the consequences.

The death of University of Maryland basketball star Len Bias and an article by Dr. Jeffery Isner in the New England Journal of Medicine that same year have established that cocaine can cause fatal heart problems. These deaths can occur regardless of whether the user has had previous heart problems and regardless of how the cocaine was taken. Cocaine users also describe its effect in sexual terms. Its intense and sensual effect makes it a stronger aphrodisiac than sex itself. Research at UCLA with apes given large amounts of cocaine showed they preferred the drug to food or sexual partners and were willing to endure severe electric shocks in exchange for large doses.

The cocaine problem in this country has been made worse by the introduction of crack: ordinary coke mixed with baking soda and water into a solution and heated. This material is then dried and broken into tiny chunks that resemble rock candy. Users usually smoke these crack rocks in glass pipes. Crack (so-called because of the cracking sound it makes when heated) has become the scourge of the war on drugs. A single hit of crack provides an intense, wrenching rush in a matter of seconds. Because crack is absorbed rapidly through the lungs and hits the brain within seconds, it is the most dangerous form of cocaine and the most addicting.

Another major difference is not physiological but economic. According to Dr. Mark Gold, founder of the nationwide cocaine hotline, the cost to an addict using crack is one-tenth the cost he would have paid for the equivalent in cocaine powder just a decade ago. Since crack costs much less than normal cocaine, it is particularly appealing to adolescents. About one in five 12th graders has tried cocaine, and that percentage is certain to increase because of the price and availability of crack.

The drug of choice during the 1960s was LSD. People looking for the "ultimate trip" would take LSD or perhaps peyote and experience bizarre illusions and hallucinations. In the last few decades, these hallucinogens have been replaced by PCP (Phencyclidine), often known as "angel dust" or "killer weed." First synthesized in the 1950s as an anesthetic, PCP was discontinued because of its side effects but is now manufactured illegally and sold to thousands of teenagers.

PCP is often sprayed on cigarettes or marijuana and then smoked. Users report a sense of distance and estrangement. PCP creates body-image distortion, dizziness, and double vision. The drug distorts reality in such a way that it can resemble mental illness. Because the drug blocks pain receptors, violent PCP episodes may result in self-inflicted injuries. Chronic PCP users have persistent memory problems and speech difficulties. Mood disorders such as depression, anxiety, and violent behavior, are also reported. High doses of PCP can produce a coma that can last for days or weeks.

The latest scourge in the drug business has been so-called designer drugs. These synthetic drugs, manufactured in underground laboratories, mimic the effects of commonly abused drugs.

Since they were not even anticipated when our current drug laws were written, they exist in a legal limbo, and their use is increasing. One drug is MDMA, also know as "Ecstasy." It has been called the "LSD of the '80s" and gives the user a cocaine-like rush with a hallucinogen euphoria. Ecstasy was sold legally for a few years despite National Institute on Drug Abuse fears that it could cause brain damage. In 1985 the DEA outlawed MDMA, although it is still widely available. Other drugs have been marketed as a variation of the painkillers Demerol and Fentanyl. The synthetic variation of the anesthetic Fentanyl is considered more potent than heroin and is known on the street as "synthetic heroin" and "China White." Designer drugs may become a growth industry in the '90s. Creative drug makers in clandestine laboratories can produce these drugs for a fraction of the cost of smuggled drugs and with much less hassle from law enforcement agencies.

24.8% of students had smoked a whole cigarette before 13 years of age. Male students (28.0%) were significantly more likely than female students (20.9%) to have smoked a whole cigarette before 13 years of age. White students (25.6%) and Hispanic students (24.9%) were significantly more likely than black students (17.4%) to have smoked a whole cigarette before 13 years of age. Students in grades 9 (32.0%) and 10 (27.5%) were significantly more likely than students in grades 11 (22.2%) and 12 (18.6%) to have smoked a whole cigarette before 13 years of age.

36.4% of students had smoked cigarettes on >1 of the 30 days preceding the survey (i.e., current cigarette use). White students (39.7%) were significantly more likely than Hispanic students (34.0%) and black students (22.7%) to report current cigarette use. Hispanic students (34.0%) were significantly more likely than black students (22.7%) to report current cigarette use.

16.7% of students had smoked cigarettes on > 20 of the 3days preceding the survey (i.e., frequent cigarette use). White students (19.9%) were significantly more likely than Hispanic students (10.9%) and black students (7.1%) to report frequent cigarette use.

9.3% of students had used smokeless tobacco (chewing tobacco or snuff) on >1 of the 30 days preceding the survey. Male students (15.8%) were significantly more likely than female students (1.5%) to have used smokeless tobacco. White students (12.2%) were significantly more likely than Hispanic students (5.1%) and black students (2.2%) to have used smokeless tobacco.

9.8% of students (<18 years of age who reported current cigarette use) had purchased their cigarettes in a store or gas station during the 30 days preceding the survey. Students in grades 11 (36.7%) and 12 (43.5%) were significantly more likely than students in grades

9 (17.8%) and 10 (25.7%) to purchase cigarettes in a store or gas station.

Among students reporting current cigarette use, 66.7% of those <18 years of age who purchased cigarettes in a store or gas station had not been asked to show proof of age. Students in grade 9 (82.8%) were significantly more likely than students in grades 11 (59.8%) and 12 (54.9%) not to have been asked to show proof of age.

79.1% of students had had at least one drink of alcohol during their lifetime. Hispanic students (83.1%) and white students (81.3%) were significantly more likely than black students (73.0%) to have had at least one drink of alcohol during their lifetime. Students in grades 11 (81.9%) and 12 (84.0%) were significantly more likely than students in grade 9 (72.0%) to have had at least one drink of alcohol during their lifetime.

50.8% of students had had at least one drink of alcohol on > 1 of the 30 days preceding the survey (i.e., current alcohol use). White students (54.0%) and Hispanic students (53.9%) were significantly more likely than black students (36.9%) to report current alcohol use. Students in grade 12 (57.3%) were significantly more likely than students in grades 9 (44.2%) and 10 (47.2%) to report current alcohol use.

33.4% of students had had five or more drinks of alcohol on > 1 occasions during the 30 days preceding the survey (i.e., episodic heavy drinking). Male students (37.3%) were significantly more likely than female students (28.6%) to report episodic heavy drinking. White students (37.7%) and Hispanic students (34.9%) were significantly more likely than black students (16.1%) to report episodic heavy drinking. Students in grades 11 (37.5%) and 12 (39.3%) were significantly more likely than students in grades 9 (25.7%) and 10 (29.9%) to report episodic heavy drinking. Initiation of Risk Behaviors In 1997, as part of the Youth Risk Behavior Surveillance System, the Centers for Disease Control and Prevention conducted a national school-based Youth Risk Behavior Survey that resulted in 16,262 questionnaires completed by students in 151 schools. These data are summarized from that survey. For more information see CDC, Youth Risk Behavior Surveillance – United States, 1997. MMWR 1998;47 (N 31.1% of students had first drunk alcohol (more than a few sips) before 13 years of age. Male students (35.7%) were significantly more likely than female students (25.7%) to have drunk alcohol before 13 years of age. Hispanic students (37.9%) were significantly more likely than white students (28.8%) to have drunk alcohol before 13 years of age. Students in grade 9 (41.9%) were significantly more likely than students in grades 10 (32.0%), 11 (29.9%), and 12 (22.8%) to have drunk alcohol before 13 years of age. Students in grades 10 (32.0%) and 11 (29.9%) were significantly more likely than students in grade 12 (22.8%) to have drunk alcohol before 13 years of age.

9.7% of students had tried marijuana before 13 years of age. Male students (12.2%) were significantly more likely than female students (6.7%) to have tried marijuana before 13 years of age. Hispanic students (13.2%) were significantly more likely than white students (7.5%) to have tried marijuana before 13 years of age. Students in grade 9 (14.9%) were significantly more likely than students in grades 11 (8.3%) and 12 (5.8%) to have tried marijuana before 13 years of age. Students in grade 10 (10.4%) were significantly more likely than students in grade 12 (5.8%) to have tried marijuana before 13 years of age.

1.1% of students had tried cocaine (including powder, "crack" or "freebase" forms of cocaine) before 13 years of age Hispanic students (1.4%) were significantly more likely than black students (0.4%) to have tried cocaine before 13 years of age.

Chapter Twenty Six - Conclusion

My trips to Africa were among the many gifts of recovery. Today, after fifteen and a half continuous years of abstinence from drugs and alcohol, I continue to work on tolerance and patience—with myself, and others. I'm especially annoyed with people talking through meetings, showing no respect for the urgency of the message however I remind myself that there were days when I was and am disruptive as well so I try not to criticize, condemn or judge anyone. We're all in this together.

I'm still not in a committed relationship but I trust God and His will. As long as He is the ultimate authority ALL will be well. Everything happens on His schedule, not mine.

I am, however, involved in community affairs and civil and human rights issues. For five years, I promised myself, and others, that I would write my story. The day finally came. I started the journey of writing, reminding myself that inch-by-inch anything's a cinch. I've been at it since August 2005 and it's now October 2006. It feels wonderful to actually accomplish something that I started. All of my life I've always started many projects, never finishing any.

I remember the many Christmases when I was so sure that I knew how to put the bikes together. The directions were too long and complicated. "I can do this without all of the confusion and complication of the directions," I thought. Because I didn't follow the process, the wheels were always wobbly, the screws always in the wrong places and you had to pedal the damn thing backwards to make it go. In reality, my approach was always a health hazard and indicative of how I lived my life.

I'm so grateful that my life has been what it has. I wouldn't change a thing because it has made me what I am today. I would not wish to take away any of the shame, guilt, the pain, or one tear. I'll always be eternally grateful to God that I wasn't exposed to integration—the worse curse suffered by Blacks since coming to America—and that I was schooled by loving, caring, and nurturing Black people. I'm thankful to God that in His divine providence, and His book of Life, He didn't allow me to suffer the perils and trauma of integration. Even as I express gratitude to have grown up in a segregated South, I realize some of my brothers and sisters bear the mark of that racist period in our history differently.

If any of this book sounds racist, it's not. It's truth as I see it and history confirms it. Yet, as I reflect on my life and experiences, I have to remember that it was a white man that dark night on Highway 74 who repaired my car and refused payment. It was a white man who invited me into his fabulous office on Park Avenue in the early 60s and gave me not just a chance in the way of a job, but most importantly, respect. He also treated me with more kindness than I had ever been shown in my entire life by another human being at that time. Lastly, it was a white man who saved my life from the perils of addiction, taught me how to love again, how to live again, and nurtured me more than anyone I know. I'll always be truly grateful to him because I love him more than a brother.

There are no coincidences in life. God is the author and the finisher of all that was, that is, and that will be. I will always believe that God sent these men to intercede in my life and to teach me that we're all His children. They gave me nothing short of Biblical love. Each modeled the beatitudes we all know: Remember to "love ye one another as I have loved you." (John 15:12) "You are your brothers keeper." (Genesis 4:9) And "In as much as ye have done it unto one of the least of these my brethren, ye have done it unto me." (Matthew 5:19)

I know there are many good white people who abhor the evils of racism and satanic treatment Blacks have endured in this society for ages however their silence is deafening. Silence is and always will be a sign of condoning, a form of silent approval.

Because of systems in place to keep Black families apart, men find it easy to leave their wives and children. While women accept the role of sole provider, their anger at being forced to do so is real. It is no wonder that some black women do not easily trust some black men to lead their households. There some children who do not know their fathers. We do not have to stretch imagination to see why all the addictions I named earlier are prevalent in our society.

As for some of my brothers, we know that sometimes we have failed our women and children because of the enormous psychological and spiritual trauma suffered every moment of our lives in this society whether we admit it or not. then there are brothers and sisters whose family rearing and backgrounds were more stable and blessed with stronger role models who have done exceptional jobs with their children and spouses. God bless you,you indeed are some of the role models needed in this new village appearing soon. Our brothers are the subject of fear by white men and women because we represent to them some type of threat. I can't imagine why because we're the same ones who saved your ancestors lives in past wars. We are oppressed in the workforce, unable to live our fullest potential. These psychological, emotional, and spiritual traumas devastate. We finally reach for anything to ease the pain, if only momentarily.

In most cases that something is of a mood altering, mind changing substance. Racism affects the white race as well. While it may be covert, some of their children are collectively taught this demonic system from birth. Institutional racism slowly, insipidly transforms these children into the demons they deny exists. Because of their privileged expectations, when denied, they exact their rage and vengeance on society, their own parents, and school mates. Because the media doesn't report on white dysfunction, a few years ago, U.S. News ran a story entitled: "A Shocking Look at Blacks and Crime." Yet never have they or any other news outlet discussed the "shocking" whiteness of these shoot-em-ups. Indeed, every time media commentators discuss the similarities in these crimes they mention that the shooters were boys, they were loners, they got picked on, but never do they seem to notice a certain highly visible melanin deficiency. Color-blind, I guess.

Inherent in man is a spiritual nature that only God can fill. When that void is not filled with that which is spiritual, we reach for something, anything to fill the emptiness in our souls. That something can be a substance such as alcohol, drugs, nicotine; material things (houses, cars, clothes, jewelry), it can be prestige, power, sex, gambling, eating, or an enormous craving for attention. These are called addictors which lead to addiction and can be deadly. These addictions draw us farther into the abyss that leads to hopelessness, depression, and insanity. We are people caught in the grip of a spiritual and emotional dilemma, the solution of which is spiritual in nature.

I bear witness to the prophets, the apostles and the saints that there is but one God who is called by many names. He allows His rain to fall on the just and the unjust whose mercies are never-ending, and whose compassion and grace are everlasting. As long as He is the ultimate authority all will be well. All praises to Him for this new dawning and revelation in my life. I will wash the feet of my brothers, sisters, fathers, mothers, and children with His love.

As I sat on that Cape Coast years ago at night listening to the nearby villagers sing their beautiful and happy songs of worship and praise, I became very emotional. They never lost their identity, their customs, their native tongues, or their religious beliefs. Because of that they're happy with themselves and others.

As I gazed up into God's Heavens and saw the brilliant full moon, the stars, and galaxies, the tears started flowing from the immense joy that I felt in my heart, and the love that I have for my beloved Black people. I couldn't help but reminisce about the hell that I had lived for thirty-two years. I thought to myself, "look at me now GOD. Are you proud of me? LOOK AT ME NOW, ARE YOU PROUD OF ME? I'M FREE AT LAST, FREE AT LAST, GREAT GOD ALMIGHTY, I'M FREE AT LAST!"

"Do you solemnly swear that the testimony you are about to give this court is the truth, the whole truth and nothing but the truth so help you God?"

"I just did."

Asante Sana Osei

APPENDIX

The following is a list of notable people who have died from drug-related causes. It includes deaths caused by alcohol and caffeine.

Dave Alexander - of The Stooges
Rick Allen - of Asylum
G.G. Allin - punk musician, heroin
West Arkeen - of Outpatience, and songwriter, heroin
Howard Arkley - painter
Arlus - of the Blunt Stitches
Deford Bailey - country musician
Chet Baker - ~~jazz~~ trumpeter and singer
Florence Ballard - of The Supremes, cardiac arrest strongly exacerbated by long-term drug abuse
Honoré de Balzac - caffeine poisoning from drinking over forty cups of coffee a day
Lester Bangs - musician, writer, overdose of painkillers, possibly accidental
Jean-Michel Basquiat - painter
Ludwig van Beethoven - classical musician, note: alcohol abuse led to the serious health problems that caused his death
Bix Beiderbecke - jazz musician
Len Bias, college basketball star
Elisa Bridges, Playboy Playmate

Tim Buckley, musician John Belushi - of the Blues Brothers, actor, and comedian - heroin and cocaine

Bunny Berigan

Sonny Berman - jazz musician

Wes Berggren - of Tripping Daisy

Len Bias - basketball star; died of cocaine overdose before ever playing in the NBA

Dave Bidwell - of the Pink Fairies, Chicken Shack, Savoy Brown

Matty Blag - of Blaggers I.T.A

Mike Bloomfield - blues guitarist, heroin

Tommy Bolin - of Deep Purple

John Bonham - of Led Zeppelin, inhalation of own vomit; believed to be alcohol-related

James Booker - musician, heroin

Erik Brodreskift - of Borknagar

Herman Brood - musician

Dennis Brown - musician

Lenny Bruce - comedian, heroin, found dead with a needle in his arm

Robert Buck - of 10,000 Maniacs

Tim Buckley - rock and roll musician, heroin

Lester Butler - harpist, of the Red Devils, heroin

Paul Butterfield - American blues musician

Toy Caldwell - of Marshall Tucker Band

Alex Campbell - musician

Skip Candelori - of Turning Point

Gia Carangi, supermodel

Herb Caro - saxophoneist, clarinetist, heroin

Leroy Carr - blues musician

Miss Christine - of the GTOs

Michael Clarke - of the Byrds

Steve Clarke - of Def Leppard

Will Clay - of The Toys

Montgomery Clift - actor

Kurt Cobain - Nirvana singer and guitarist, heroin and gunshot wounds

Brian Cole - of the Association

Allen Collins - of Lynyrd Skynyrd
Cowboy - of Grandmaster Flash & the Furious Five;
Carl Crack - of Atari Teenage Riot
Darby Crash - punk musician, of the Germs, heroin
Todd Crew - of the Drunk Fux and Jetboy
Robbin Crosby - of Ratt, contracted HIV as a result of long-time heroin addiction and died of AIDS
Dalida - singer, barbiturates
Dorothy Dandridge - actress, singer
Jesse Ed Davis - guitarist, session musician, heroin
Jeanine Deckers - the Singing Nun
Sheik Sayid Darwish, Egyptian composer and father of Arab popular music, cocaine
Rick Dey - of the Vejtables, February Sunshine, the Wilde Knights and the Merry-Go-Round
DJ Screw - musician, codeine
Tommy Dorsey - jazz musician and bandleader, choked to death while sleeping with the aid of drugs
John Dougherty - of Flipper
Nick Drake - musician
Bobby Driscoll - actor
Jeanne Eagels - actress
John Entwistle – musician of the Who
Brian Epstein - Beatles manager
Rick Evers - drummer and songwriter
Hollywood Fats - musician
Chris Farley - comedian, actor
Pete Farnden - of the Pretenders
Rainer Werner Fassbinder - playwright, director
W.C. Fields - American performer and actor
Keith Ferguson - of the Fabulous Thunderbirds
Zach Foley - of EMF and Carrie
Tom Foote - of the Devices and the Loco Gringos
Rory Gallagher - of Taste
Jerry Garcia - of the Grateful Dead, cardiac arrest strongly exacerbated by longtime heroin abuse
Paul Gardiner - of Gary Numan's Tubeway Army

Judy Garland - American actress
Duck Geottel - of Skinny Puppy, heroin
Andy Gibb - singer, younger brother of the Bee Gees; cardiac damage strongly exacerbated by cocaine and alcohol abuse
Candy Givens - of Zephyr
Trevor Goddard, actor
Alexander Godunov - Actor, died of alcoholism at 45
Dwayne Goettel - heroin
Gribouille (1941-1968), French singer
Stacy Guess - of the Squirrel Nut Zippers
Paul Hammond - of Atomic Rooster
Bobby Hatfield - of the Righteous Brothers, heart attack triggered by cocaine overdose
Tim Hardin - heroin
Wynonie Harris - blues singer, alcohol poisoning
George Harrison - of the Beatles, heavy tobacco user, died of lung cancer
Alex Harvey - of The Sensational Alex Harvey Band, liver damage caused by alcohol abuse
Eddie Hazel - guitarist, of the P-funk collective
Helno - of Les Negresses Vertes
Margaux Hemingway - actress
Jimi Hendrix - rock and roll musician, respiratory arrest caused by barbiturate overdose
Gregory Herbet - of Blood, Sweat & Tears;
Bob Hite - of Canned Heat
Randy Jo Hobbs - musician
El Duce Hoke - of the Mentors
Michael Holiday - singer
Billie Holiday - jazz singer
Gary Holton - of Heavy Metal Kids
James Honeyman-Scott - of the Pretenders
Shannon Hoon - of Blind Melon
Tim Hovey - actor
Baby Huey - singer
Phyllis Hyman - singer

Bobby Hatfield, musician (fatal heart attack was triggered by a cocaine overdose)
Shannon Hoon, musician
Lorri Jackson - musician
Tom Jans - musician
Joëlle (1953-1982), American born French singer
Brian Jones - of the Rolling Stones, drowned, very likely due to alcohol and barbiturate intoxication
Rob Jones - of Wonder Stuff
Janis Joplin - rock and roll and blues musician, heroin
John Kahn - of the Jerry Garcia Band
Jeff Kaplan - of Kaleidoscope
Wells Kelly - of Orleans
Beverly Kenney - singer
Kenny Kirkland - noted pianist, heroin
Hoi Klinskih - of Sector Gaza
Paul Kossoff - of Free
Lance Krantz - drummer of Detox
Eddie Kurdziel - of Redd Kross
Peter Laughner - of Pere Ubu; acute pancreatitis
Rudy Lewis - of the Drifters
Bela Lugosi- actor
Frankie Lymon - doo wop singer, heroin
Sonny Liston - world champion boxer (possible)
Phil Lynott - of Thin Lizzy
Steve MacKay
Billy MacKenzie - of the Associates
Mike MacTavish - of the Lost Souls
Steve Marriott - of The Small Faces and Humble Pie, drug related fire
Big Maybelle
Jad McAdam - of Lino
David McComb - of Traffic
David McComb (no relation) - of The Triffids
Jimmy McCulloch - guitarist
Pig Pen McKernan - of the Grateful Dead
Robbie McIntosh - of the Average White Band, heroin

Clyde McPhatter - singer
Joe Meek - record producer
Jonathan Melvoin - touring keyboardist for the Smashing Pumpkins, heroin
Mighty Spoiler - calypso music singer
Miss Christine - of the GTO's
Amedeo Modigliani - painter, alcohol poisoning
Marilyn Monroe - actress, singer
Ken Montgomery - of D.O.A
Roy Montrell - session guitarist
Keith Moon - of the Who
Jim Morrison - of the Doors, heroin and alcohol (cause and fact of death disputed)
Billy Murcia - of the New York Dolls
Brent Mydland - keyboardist, of the Grateful Dead
Papoose Nelson - blues musician
Jerry Nolan - of The New York Dolls and The Heartbreakers
Bradley Nowell - of Sublime, heroin
Hugh O'Connor - actor, of In the Heat of the Night TV series
Lani O'Grady - actress, of Eight Is Enough
Frank O'Keefe - of the Outlaws
Johnny O'Keefe - singer
Brian O'Leary - actor
Charlie Ondras - of Unsane
Malcolm Owen - singer, lyricist of the Ruts
Marco Pantani - cyclist, Tour de France winner; acute cocaine intoxication
Charlie Parker - jazz musician
Robert Pastorelli - American television actor
Gram Parsons - country musician, of the Byrds and the Flying Burrito Brothers
Joe Pass - jazz musician
Jon-Jon Paulos - of the Buckinghams
Art Pepper - jazz musician
Kristen Pfaff - of Hole, heroin
Esther Phillips - singer
John Phillips - musician, of the Mamas and the Papas

River Phoenix - actor
Jeffrey Lee Pierce - of the Gun Club
Rob Pilatus - of Milli Vanilli
Dana Plato - actress, of Diff'rent Strokes
Elvis Presley - singer
Freddie Prinze - comic, actor (Chico and the Man), self-inflicted gunshot wound while under the influence of Quaaludes
Karen Ann Quinlan put into an extreme vegetative state by tranquilizers and alcohol died, 1985,
Glenn Quinn - actor (Roseanne, Angel)
Robert Quine - punk rock guitarist
Dee Dee Ramone - of the Ramones
Alex Ramsdell - jaz pianist
Johnny Ray - musician
Wallace Reid - actor
Elis Regina - singer
Rob Graves Ritter - of Thelonius Monster, Gun Club, the Bags, 45 Grave
Peter Rosen - War
Michael Rudetski - keyboardist, Culture Club
David Ruffin - of the Temptations
Stefanie Sargent - of 7 Year Bitch
Bon Scott - of AC/DC, inhalation of own vomit
George Scott III - bass guitarist
Phil Seaman - singer
Jean Seberg - actress
Edie Sedgewick - actress
Will Shatter - of Flipper, heroin
Eddy Shaver - of Shaver
Bobby Sheehan - of Blues Traveler
Judee Sill - musician
Hillel Slovak - of Red Hot Chili Peppers, heroin
Richard Sohl - of The Patti Smith Group
Epic Soundtracks - of Swell Maps
Layne Staley - of Alice in Chains
Willian Stewart - doo wop singer, of Johnny Bragg & the Prisonaires

Bob Stinson - of the Replacements
Neil Storey - of the Dragon
Rory Storm - musician
Screaming Lord Sutch - singer, Prozac
Dallas Taylor - of the Danderliers
Vinnie Taylor - of Sha Na Na, heroin
Gary Thain - of Uriah Heep
Johnny Thunders - of the New York Dolls, alcohol and methadone
Dylan Thomas - poet, "an alcoholic insult to the brain."
Georg Trakl - playwright
Steven James Turner - of Clock DVA
Dick Twardzick - pianist
Lupe Vélez, actress
Sid Vicious - of the Sex Pistols, heroin
Gene Vincent - rock and roll musician, liver damage caused by alcohol
Dave Waller - musician
Dinah Washington - singer
Freddie Webster - jazz trumpeter
Brett Whiteley - painter
Keith Whitley - country musician, alcohol poisoning
Danny Whitten - of Crazy Horse, heroin
Hank Williams - country musician, overdose of painkillers, born with painful back deformation
Alan Wilson - of Canned Heat
Dennis Wilson - of the Beach Boys, exact cause of death unknown, alcohol-related drowning is a strong possibility
Andrew Wood - of Mother Love Bone

--Reprinted with permission from
The Center for Disease Control, US Government study.

About the Author

Moyo, Kwame Osei, b. 1945 Charlotte, NC as Thomas C Saunders, African American civil rights, political and community activist. He has six children, is divorced and is the President of Health Carousel of the Carolinas. He is also the CEO of Omega First Inc a non profit organization that serves the recovery community and works with recovering substance abusers. He is currently the Chairman of the Board of the Kushite Institute for Wholistic Development. He also is a member of The Color of Change Org, Democracy Now, The Move On org, NAACP and N'Cobra. He served as scoutmaster with the Boy Scouts of America for over six years. He has lectured on substance abuse at the University of Winneba located in Winneba Ghana West Africa. He himself is a recovering addict with almost sixteen years clean time. He says with humor that he received his doctorate Degree from UCLA (Under the Corner of Lenox Avenue)

Printed in the United States
66669LVS00005B/253-468